OFFICIAL
SQA
PAST
PAPERS
WITH ANSWERS

**INTERMEDIATE 2**

# FRENCH
## 2007-2011

SQA

BrightRED
PUBLISHING

**Publisher's Note**

We are delighted to bring you the 2011 Past Papers and you will see that we have changed the format from previous editions. As part of our environmental awareness strategy, we have attempted to make these new editions as sustainable as possible.

To do this, we have printed on white paper and bound the answer sections into the book. This not only allows us to use significantly less paper but we are also, for the first time, able to source all the materials from sustainable sources.

We hope you like the new editions and by purchasing this product, you are not only supporting an independent Scottish publishing company but you are also, in the International Year of Forests, not contributing to the destruction of the world's forests.

Thank you for your support and please see the following websites for more information to support the above statement –

www.fsc-uk.org

www.loveforests.com

© Scottish Qualifications Authority
All rights reserved. Copying prohibited. No part of this publication may be reproduced, stored in a retrieval system, or transmitted in any form or by any means, electronic, mechanical, photocopying, recording or otherwise.

First exam published in 2007.
Published by Bright Red Publishing Ltd, 6 Stafford Street, Edinburgh EH3 7AU
tel: 0131 220 5804 fax: 0131 220 6710 info@brightredpublishing.co.uk  www.brightredpublishing.co.uk

ISBN 978-1-84948-198-4

A CIP Catalogue record for this book is available from the British Library.

Bright Red Publishing is grateful to the copyright holders, as credited on the final page of the Question Section, for permission to use their material. Every effort has been made to trace the copyright holders and to obtain their permission for the use of copyright material.
Bright Red Publishing will be happy to receive information allowing us to rectify any error or omission in future editions.

[BLANK PAGE]

FOR OFFICIAL USE

| | | | | | |
|---|---|---|---|---|---|
| | | | | | |

Mark

# X059/201

NATIONAL
QUALIFICATIONS
2007

THURSDAY, 17 MAY
9.00 AM – 10.10 AM

## FRENCH
### INTERMEDIATE 2
Reading

---

**Fill in these boxes and read what is printed below.**

Full name of centre

Town

Forename(s)

Surname

Date of birth
Day   Month   Year     Scottish candidate number     Number of seat

When you are told to do so, open your paper and write your answers **in English** in the spaces provided.

You may use a French dictionary.

Before leaving the examination room you must give this book to the invigilator. If you do not, you may lose all the marks for this paper.

SCOTTISH
QUALIFICATIONS
AUTHORITY

©

*Points*

You would like to work in France and you look on the Internet for some information about jobs.

**1.** You see this job advert.

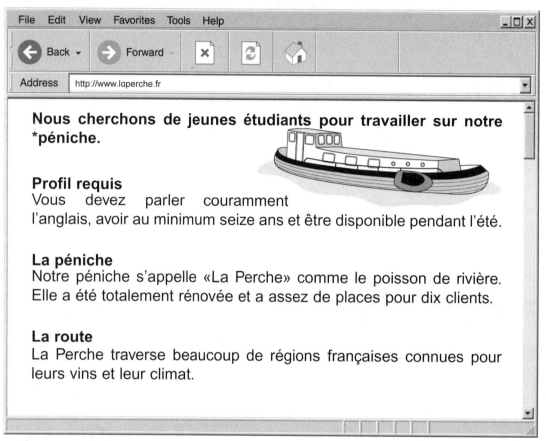

*une péniche = barge/canal boat

(*a*)  According to the title, what type of people should apply for this job?    **1**

Students who are still studying

(*b*)  What requirements must you have to be able to apply for the job? Mention any **two** things.    **2**

to be able to speak good English

and to be over 16

(*c*)  Mention any **one** detail about the barge "La Perche".    **1**

It was named after a fish

(*d*)  The barge passes through many regions of France. What **two** things are they famous for?    **1**

for its wine & climate/weather

[X059/201]                              *Page two*

*Points*

**2.** You are interested in this job and you read on to find out more.

**Vos tâches**
Vous serez responsable du nettoyage des cabines et des visites guidées à chaque *escale.

**Vos horaires**
Vous travaillerez six heures par jour, cinq jours par semaine.

**Les loisirs**
Pendant votre temps libre vous pourrez descendre pour marcher le long du canal ou si vous préférez, vous pourrez rester à bord pour faire de la lecture.

**L'hébergement et les repas**
Vous partagerez votre cabine avec deux autres personnes. A bord il y a une petite cuisine toute équipée pour préparer les repas.

*une escale = port of call/stop

(*a*)  Which **two** tasks will you be responsible for?  2

tour Guids

and Cabin cleaning

(*b*)  How long will you work **per week**?  1

Work of 30 hows weekly

(*c*)  What can you do during your free time, if you get off the barge?  1

_____

(*d*)  What details are you given about the facilities on board?  Mention any **one** thing.  1

Walk down the river

**[Turn over**

DO NOT
WRITE IN
THIS
MARGIN

*Points*

**3.** You read an article in a French magazine in which two young people give their views on the venue chosen for the Olympic Games of 2012.

## Les Jeux Olympiques de 2012

Deux jeunes Parisiens donnent leur avis.

### Farid — 21 ans

Moi je suis très content que Paris n'organise pas les Jeux Olympiques.

Les Jeux Olympiques coûtent cher car il faut construire des stades, de nouvelles routes et des logements pour les athlètes. De plus, les Jeux Olympiques créent plus de circulation dans la ville. Bon courage Londres.

### Christine — 16 ans

Moi, au contraire, je suis triste que Paris n'organise pas les Jeux Olympiques.

Les Jeux Olympiques encouragent les jeunes à pratiquer un sport, créent de nombreux emplois et cela renforce l'amitié entre les pays participants.

**Farid**

(a) Farid says that the Olympic Games cost a lot of money. Why? Mention any **two** things.

2

*Because it costs to build the stations & Running tracks*

(b) What other disadvantage does he mention?

1

*It causes traffic jams and congestion.*

**Christine**

(c) Christine would have been happy for Paris to host the Olympic Games. Why? Mention any **two** things.

2

*Encourages children to practice sports & creates more jobs.*

[Turn over for Question 4 on *Pages six, seven* and *eight*

**4.** You read another article about things that annoy people in today's society.

# Ça m'énerve

Beaucoup de choses dans la société moderne améliorent notre vie de tous les jours, par exemple on peut acheter ses courses par Internet, communiquer avec ses amis par ordinateur et aller à l'étranger pour moins de cinq euros. Mais sommes-nous toujours satisfaits de ces changements?

Il paraît que non! Deux jeunes gens parlent de ce qui les énerve.

### Sylvie — 20 ans

Dans notre société moderne la protection de l'environnement est une des choses dont on parle le plus, pourtant les gens continuent à utiliser leur voiture dans les centres-villes. **Et ça, ça m'énerve!**

Les gens ne veulent pas utiliser les bus car ils disent que les bus sont souvent surchargés, sales et en retard. Mais pourquoi ne pas aller en ville à pied ou en vélo? Par exemple mon père ne se déplace qu'en vélo pour aller au travail. Non seulement le vélo est un moyen de transport propre mais il permet aussi de faire de l'exercice.

Si on habite loin de son travail on peut toujours laisser sa voiture dans les grands parkings autour de la ville et puis prendre le métro. Dans ma ville, le centre est interdit aux voitures; il y a donc moins de bruit et les gens peuvent se promener sans danger.

### Thomas — 16 ans

Aujourd'hui tout le monde utilise un téléphone portable n'importe où et n'importe quand. **Et ça, ça m'énerve!!**

Il est vrai que le téléphone portable peut être très utile en cas de panne de voiture ou en cas d'urgence médicale par exemple. Mais est-il vraiment nécessaire d'utiliser son téléphone dans un restaurant pour décrire ce que l'on mange ou au supermarché pour demander ce qu'il faut acheter?

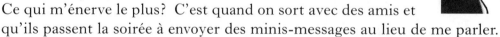

Ce qui m'énerve le plus? C'est quand on sort avec des amis et qu'ils passent la soirée à envoyer des minis-messages au lieu de me parler.

De plus le téléphone portable devrait être interdit à l'école. La sonnerie des téléphones interrompt les cours et les élèves perdent donc leur concentration et par conséquent ils ne comprennent pas forcément la leçon.

*Points*

## 4. (continued)

(a)  A lot of things improve our everyday life.  Mention any **two** examples
that are given.

2

*Contacting via email and internet*
*Shopping*

## Sylvie

(b)  What annoys Sylvie in today's modern society?

1

*That using cars in city centres effects*
*the environment.*

(c)  According to Sylvie, why do people not want to use buses?  Mention
any **two** things.

2

*They are cramped and dirty.*

(d)  Her dad goes to work by bike.  Why does Sylvie think that a bike is a
good means of transport?  Mention any **one** thing.

1

*It causes less pollution*

(e)  What does Sylvie suggest you do if you live far from your work?

2

*don't use your car, use a*
*subway / underground*

(f)  In the centre of Sylvie's town, cars are forbidden.  Mention
**one** advantage of this.

1

*less pollution in the town centre and*
*its cleaner*

## Thomas

(g)  Mobile phones can be very useful.  Mention any **one** example that
Thomas gives.

1

*They are good for emergencies such*
*as car breakdowns*

*Points*

## 4. (continued)

(*h*)  Thomas gives two examples of people using their mobile phones where it is not necessary.

In the grid below, write the reason why they use their phone in each place.

2

| Place | Reason |
|---|---|
| Restaurant | |
| Supermarket | To coh whub shopping so get |

(*i*)  What annoys Thomas most when he goes out with his friends?

1

That they go on their phones too much

(*j*)  Why does Thomas think that mobile phones should be forbidden in schools?  Mention any **two** things.

2

Pupils can loose focus and is distracting

**Total (30 points)**

**= 30 marks**

*[END OF QUESTION PAPER]*

# X059/203

NATIONAL
QUALIFICATIONS
2007

THURSDAY, 17 MAY
10.30 AM – 11.00 AM

**FRENCH
INTERMEDIATE 2**
Listening Transcript

**This paper must not be seen by any candidate.**

The material overleaf is provided for use in an emergency only (eg the recording or equipment proving faulty) or where permission has been given in advance by SQA for the material to be read to candidates with additional support needs. The material must be read exactly as printed.

SCOTTISH
QUALIFICATIONS
AUTHORITY

## Transcript—Intermediate 2

---

**Instructions to reader(s):**

For each item, read the English **once**, then read the French **twice**, with an interval of 1 minute between the two readings. On completion of the second reading, pause for the length of time indicated in brackets after each item, to allow the candidates to write their answers.

Where special arrangements have been agreed in advance to allow the reading of the material, those sections marked **(f)** should be read by a female speaker and those marked **(m)** by a male: those sections marked **(t)** should be read by the teacher.

---

**(t)**    In the summer you are working on a barge in France.

**Question number one.**

While in France you meet Maryse who comes from Lyon. She tells you about her everyday life.

**You now have one minute to study the question.**

**(f)**    Bonjour! Je m'appelle Maryse et j'habite à 5 kilomètres de Lyon avec mes parents et ma petite soeur. Je m'entends très bien avec mes parents mais ma petite soeur est très paresseuse et nous nous disputons tout le temps. Ma mère est infirmière et travaille tard, donc le soir je mets la table et je prépare le dîner. Ma mère me donne de l'argent de poche mais je veux gagner un peu plus d'argent parce que je veux aller en Espagne l'année prochaine. Donc, le week-end, je travaille comme serveuse dans un restaurant à Lyon. Ça me permet de mettre de l'argent sur mon compte en banque pour les vacances, d'acheter des vêtements et de sortir avec mes amis. Je trouve les petits boulots très utiles. Ça donne aux jeunes une première expérience du monde du travail et nous rend plus indépendants.

*(3 minutes)*

**(t)**    **Question number two.**

Maryse goes on to tell you a little more about Lyon.

**You now have one minute to study the question.**

**(f)**    Lyon est situé dans l'Est de la France et a un climat très variable. En été, par exemple, le matin il peut faire très chaud et puis à 3 heures il y a des orages. Lyon est très bien desservi par les transports avec un aéroport international à 25 kilomètres et on peut être à Paris en 2 heures avec le TGV, le train à grande vitesse qui est très confortable et rarement en retard. Comme Lyon est une ville universitaire, il y a beaucoup d'étudiants qui viennent y étudier la médecine, la politique et les langues étrangères par exemple. Lyon est aussi connu comme la capitale gastronomique française et bien manger et boire sont très importants pour les habitants. On peut y acheter de bons jambons et toutes sortes de fromage. On dit que les gens de Lyon sont froids et assez distants mais bien sûr je ne suis pas d'accord.

*(3 minutes)*

**(t)**  **Question number three.**

You then meet Rodolphe who spent some time in Scotland as a French assistant.

**You now have one minute to study the question.**

**(m)**  L'année dernière j'ai passé un an dans une école écossaise comme assistant de français. J'ai travaillé avec des petits groupes d'élèves âgés entre 11 et 17 ans. J'ai fait des cours sur la vie en France et le cinéma français.

Un des meilleurs moments de mon séjour en Ecosse était lorsque je suis allé dans le Nord de l'Ecosse avec l'école. On a logé dans une auberge de jeunesse qui était très propre et moi j'ai partagé une chambre avec un professeur d'histoire qui accompagnait le groupe. On passait les matinées à visiter des châteaux, des monuments célèbres et des distilleries de whisky. L'après-midi on faisait de belles promenades sur les plages et des randonnées en montagne. J'ai ainsi pu prendre énormément de photos. Le paysage était magnifique mais j'étais étonné par le manque d'arbres. Un des profs m'a expliqué qu'il n'y a pas beaucoup d'arbres car il y a trop de vent. Cela dit j'ai passé une année extraordinaire en Ecosse. J'ai amélioré mon anglais et j'ai rencontré des gens très sympathiques. J'espère y retourner un jour.

*(3 minutes)*

**(t)**  **End of test.**

**Now look over your answers.**

*[END OF TRANSCRIPT]*

[BLANK PAGE]

FOR OFFICIAL USE

| | | | | | |
|---|---|---|---|---|---|
| | | | | | |

Mark

# X059/202

NATIONAL
QUALIFICATIONS
2007

THURSDAY, 17 MAY
10.30 AM – 11.00 AM

**FRENCH
INTERMEDIATE 2**
Listening

---

**Fill in these boxes and read what is printed below.**

Full name of centre

Town

Forename(s)

Surname

Date of birth

Day   Month   Year     Scottish candidate number     Number of seat

When you are told to do so, open your paper.

You will hear three items in French. **Before you hear each item, you will have one minute to study the question.** You will hear each item twice, with an interval of one minute between playings, then you will have time to answer the questions about it before hearing the next item.

Write your answers, **in English**, in this book, in the appropriate spaces.

You may take notes as you are listening to the French, but only in this book.

You may **not** use a French dictionary.

You are not allowed to leave the examination room until the end of the test.

Before leaving the examination room you must give this book to the invigilator. If you do not, you may lose all the marks for this paper.

SCOTTISH
QUALIFICATIONS
AUTHORITY

DO NOT
WRITE IN
THIS
MARGIN

*Points*

In the summer you are working on a barge in France.

1. While in France you meet Maryse who comes from Lyon. She tells you about her everyday life.

   (*a*)   How far away from Lyon does Maryse live?                                                    **1**

   _____

   (*b*)   What does Maryse say about her little sister? Mention any **one** thing.    **1**

   _____

   (*c*)   What is Maryse's mother's job?                                                              **1**

   _____

   (*d*)   How does Maryse help out in the house? Mention any **one** thing.         **1**

   _____

   (*e*)   Which job does Maryse do at the weekend to earn some extra money?    **1**

   _____

   (*f*)   What does she do with the money she earns from her job? Mention any **two** things.    **2**

   _____

   _____

   (*g*)   Why does Maryse think part-time jobs are useful for young people? Mention any **one** thing.    **1**

   _____

*       *       *       *       *

*Points*

**2.**    Maryse goes on to tell you a little more about Lyon.

   (*a*)    Where exactly is Lyon situated?        **1**

_____

   (*b*)    The weather in Lyon is very variable in the summer. Complete the following sentence.

      In the morning the weather can be _____ but by 3 pm it

      can be _____ .        **1**

   (*c*)    How long does it take to go from Lyon to Paris by train?        **1**

_____

   (*d*)    What subjects can students study at the University of Lyon? Mention any **two**.        **2**

_____

_____

   (*e*)    Eating and drinking are very important to the people of Lyon. Name the **two** items of food that are mentioned.        **1**

_____

           *  *  *  *  *

**[Turn over for Question 3 on *Page four***

DO NOT
WRITE IN
THIS
MARGIN

*Points*

3.  You then meet Rodolphe who spent some time in Scotland as a French assistant.

    (*a*)  Complete the sentence.

    Rodolphe taught pupils between the ages of _____ and _____ .        **1**

    (*b*)  What did Rodolphe teach in his lessons?  Mention any **one** thing.        **1**

    _____

    (*c*)  Rodolphe went on a school trip to the north of Scotland.  Where did he stay?        **1**

    _____

    (*d*)  What did they visit in the morning?  Mention any **one** thing.        **1**

    _____

    (*e*)  What did they do in the afternoon?  Mention any **one** thing.        **1**

    _____

    (*f*)  He was surprised by the lack of trees.  What reason did a teacher give him for this?        **1**

    _____

    *        *        *        *        *

**Total (20 points)
= 20 marks**

[*END OF QUESTION PAPER*]

# X059/204

| NATIONAL QUALIFICATIONS 2007 | THURSDAY, 17 MAY 11.20 AM – 12.00 NOON | **FRENCH**<br>INTERMEDIATE 2<br>Writing |
|---|---|---|

20 marks are allocated to this paper.

You may use a French dictionary.

SCOTTISH QUALIFICATIONS AUTHORITY

You are preparing an application for the job advertised below.

| | |
|---|---|
| **Employeur:** | Hôtel les Mélèzes |
| **Poste:** | Réceptionniste |
| **Profil:** | Accueillir les clients et les renseigner sur la ville et la région. Une connaissance de la langue française est indispensable. |
| **Renseignements:** | |

Pour plus de détails sur les horaires, le salaire, l'hébergement etc.

**Contactez**

Mme Dupont,
Hôtel les Mélèzes,
Tignes.

To help you to write your application, you have been given the following checklist of information to give about yourself and to ask about the job:

- name, age, where you live
- leisure interests
- school/college career – subjects studied previously/being studied now
- reasons for application
- request for information about the job.

Make sure you deal with **all** of these points. You could also include the following information:

- any previous links with France or a French-speaking country
- work experience, if any.

You have also been given a way to start and finish this formal type of letter:

**Formal opening to letter of application**

Monsieur/Madame/Messieurs,

Suite à votre annonce, je me permets de poser ma candidature pour le poste de . . .

**Formal finish to letter of application**

En espérant que ma demande retiendra votre attention, je vous prie d'accepter, Monsieur/Madame/Messieurs, l'expression de mes sentiments distingués.

Use all of the above to help you write **in French** the letter which should be 120–150 words, excluding the formal phrases you have been given. You may use a French dictionary.

*[END OF QUESTION PAPER]*

# 2008

[BLANK PAGE]

FOR OFFICIAL USE

Mark

# X059/201

| NATIONAL QUALIFICATIONS 2008 | WEDNESDAY, 21 MAY 9.00 AM – 10.10 AM | **FRENCH** INTERMEDIATE 2 Reading |

---

**Fill in these boxes and read what is printed below.**

Full name of centre

Town

Forename(s)

Surname

Date of birth
Day  Month  Year

Scottish candidate number

Number of seat

When you are told to do so, open your paper and write your answers **in English** in the spaces provided.

You may use a French dictionary.

Before leaving the examination room you must give this book to the invigilator. If you do not, you may lose all the marks for this paper.

Question 4 is on fold-out pages 6, 7 and 8.

Points

1. You are looking for a job in a French speaking country and you find an Internet website for a company in Belgium.

Vous voulez travailler dans un environnement motivant et dynamique?

Nous recherchons des étudiant(e)s pour travailler comme
* jardiniers
* vendeurs/euses de glaces
* cuisiniers

Nous sommes une très grande compagnie avec sept parcs d'attractions en Europe et nous avons plus de quatre mille employés.

C'est l'endroit idéal pour toute la famille.  Ce n'est pas cher.  Le prix d'entrée inclut toutes les activités sauf les repas et les boissons.

(a) Which jobs are being advertised?  Mention any **two**.

   Gardening

   Cooking

2

(b) You are given information about the company.  To what do the following numbers refer?

2

| 7 | attractions |
|---|---|
| 4000 | Employees |

(c) What does the entry price include?

   Free food & drink

1

*Points*

**2.** You also find a blog where Jean-Paul, who has previously worked for the company, writes about his experiences.

```
File   Edit   View   Favorites   Tools   Help                          - □ ×
   ← Back ▾      → Forward ▾      ✗      ↻      ⌂
Address   http://www.jean-paul.fr                                          ▾
```

## Jean-Paul blog

Quand j'avais dix-neuf ans j'ai travaillé au «Parc d'Etoile» pendant les vacances de Pâques.

Quelquefois je me déguisais* en «lapin» et je distribuais des bonbons et des oeufs en chocolat aux enfants. C'était rigolo mais je n'aimais pas mon costume. Il était trop lourd. J'avais toujours soif.

Je devais aussi faire les annonces, par exemple «Le restaurant italien est ouvert à partir de midi» et «Le parc ferme dans quinze minutes».

Ce que j'aimais le plus c'était les bons rapports entre collègues.

**\*Se déguiser = to dress up as**

*(a)* When did Jean-Paul work at the "Parc d'Etoile"? Mention any **one** thing.      1

When he was 19

*(b)* Sometimes, as part of his job, he wore a rabbit costume. What did he have to do? Mention any **one** thing.      1

Distribute chocolate eggs to children

*(c)* What did he not like about his costume? Mention any **one** thing.      1

It was very heavy

*(d)* He also had to make announcements. Give **one** example of this.      1

The park closes in 15 minutes

*(e)* What did he like most about his work?      1

Points

3. While working in Belgium you read a magazine article in which pupils write about their school.

## Coup de Chapeau!*

**Philippe**

Chez nous, les élèves peuvent mettre des suggestions dans une boîte qu'on a installée dans chaque classe. Par conséquent : On a un menu plus sain et on peut utiliser les salles d'informatique le dimanche.

**Maryse**

Nous avons des cours de politesse pour apprendre à bien vivre ensemble et pour décourager la violence. Par exemple dans les bus on devrait laisser sa place à une personne âgée, dire bonjour au chauffeur et ne pas jeter son ticket par terre.

**\*Coup de Chapeau! = Great Idea!**

(a) In Philippe's school the pupils have suggestion boxes. What changes have been made? Mention **two** things.

2

_____

_____

*Points*

## 3. (continued)

(b) In Maryse's school they give lessons in politeness. Why? Mention any **one** thing.

It discourages violence ✓

1

(c) How should the pupils behave on buses? Mention any **two** things.

Say hello to the bus driver and thankyou for the ticket ✗

2

1

[Turn over for Question 4 on *Pages six, seven* and *eight*

**4.** You read an article about voluntary work in the magazine.

---

### Comment aider les animaux ou les gens moins chanceux que vous ?

Il y a des milliers de façons d'être bénévole*. Entraîner une équipe de foot, travailler avec les animaux malades ou visiter les personnes handicapées etc. En plus de la satisfaction, le bénévolat* vous apporte une première expérience dans le monde du travail.

Deux jeunes gens parlent de ce qu'ils font en tant que bénévoles.

#### Yannick

Moi depuis tout petit, j'ai toujours voulu un chien mais ma mère était contre. Elle disait toujours — qui va promener le chien quand il pleut? Où va-t-on laisser le chien lorsqu'on part en vacances ?

Donc j'ai décidé d'adopter un chien. Chaque mois j'envoie sept euros qui payent son logement et sa nourriture. En retour je reçois des cartes d'anniversaire et des autocollants, c'est génial. Et puis un jour j'ai lu un article dans le journal qui demandait des volontaires pour travailler avec les animaux abandonnés. J'y travaille donc depuis dix ans maintenant. On s'occupe d'oiseaux, de chats, de cobayes, de chiens etc. On leur donne à manger, nettoie leur cage et joue avec eux. En ce moment je suis à l'université pour faire des études de vétérinaire pour pouvoir un jour soigner les animaux.

#### Aisha

Il y a deux ans j'ai fait un échange scolaire au Mali*. J'étais bouleversée par la pauvreté de ce pays. Il n'y avait pas d'eau courante, les enfants étaient dans des classes de cinquante élèves et beaucoup de gens étaient malades car il n'y avait pas beaucoup de docteurs.

En rentrant en France, j'ai décidé d'être bénévole pour l'UNICEF*. On fait beaucoup de choses comme vendre des produits Unicef dans les grandes villes de France et on organise aussi des spectacles et des événements sportifs. L'argent collecté aide à construire des hôpitaux, nourrir les enfants et créer des écoles dans les villages.

De plus les élèves de mon lycée envoient des vêtements, des livres et des jouets aux enfants maliens. L'année prochaine je vais aller à la fac pour étudier la médecine car j'aimerais être médecin dans le Tiers Monde.

---

* **bénévole** = a volunteer          ***le bénévolat** = voluntary work

* **Mali**       = a country in Africa     * **UNICEF**      = a fund-raising organisation for children

Points

DO NOT
WRITE IN
THIS
MARGIN

## 4. (continued)

(a)  This article gives you some examples of voluntary work.  Mention any **two**.    2

*Work with sick animals and visit handy-capped people.*

(b)  Apart from satisfaction, what other benefit will voluntary work bring you?    1

*It will give you work experience*

## Yannick talks about his love for animals.

(c)  Yannick's mum was against having a dog.  What did she always say?  Mention any **one** thing.    1

*Who will look after the dog when on holiday.*

(d)  Yannick pays seven euros to adopt a dog.  What does this money pay for?  Mention any **one** thing.    1

*A birth certificate*

(e)  What does Yannick receive in return from his adopted dog?  Mention any **one** thing.    1

(f)  How long has Yannick been working with animals which have been abandoned?    1

*10 years*

(g)  Mention any **two** things he has to do for the abandoned animals.    2

*He feeds them & cleans their cages*

*Points*

## 4. (continued)

**Aisha talks about her visit to Mali, a country in Africa.**

(*h*) Aisha was upset by the poverty in Mali. Mention any **two** examples she gives.

2

*No money, water and there are classes of 50 kids*

(*i*) What does UNICEF do to raise money? Mention any **one** thing.

1

(*j*) What is the money collected by UNICEF used for? Mention any **two** things.

2

*It builds Hospitals and schools*

(*k*) How do the pupils in Aisha's school help the children in Mali? Mention any **one** thing.

1

$\dfrac{21}{30}$  B-

**Total (30 points)**

**= 30 marks**

*[END OF QUESTION PAPER]*

# X059/203

NATIONAL
QUALIFICATIONS
2008

WEDNESDAY, 21 MAY
10.30 AM – 11.00 AM

FRENCH
INTERMEDIATE 2
Listening Transcript

**This paper must not be seen by any candidate.**

The material overleaf is provided for use in an emergency only (eg the recording or equipment proving faulty) or where permission has been given in advance by SQA for the material to be read to candidates with additional support needs. The material must be read exactly as printed.

Transcript—Intermediate 2

---

**Instructions to reader(s):**

For each item, read the English **once**, then read the French **twice**, with an interval of 1 minute between the two readings. On completion of the second reading, pause for the length of time indicated in brackets after each item, to allow the candidates to write their answers.

Where special arrangements have been agreed in advance to allow the reading of the material, those sections marked **(f)** should be read by a female speaker and those marked **(m)** by a male: those sections marked **(t)** should be read by the teacher.

---

**(t)    Question number one.**

You have arrived in Belgium to work in an amusement park.

**You now have one minute to study the question.**

**(f)    Bonsoir et bienvenue en Belgique. Je m'appelle Michelle Durand D-U-R-A-N-D et je suis la responsable du personnel. C'est moi que vous contactez si vous avez des questions. Comme vous savez vous travaillerez 35 heures par semaine avec deux jours de congé. Vous recevrez 8 euros de l'heure avec l'hébergement et les repas compris. Vous partagerez un chalet à trois chambres avec une petite cuisine qui est très pratique pour préparer le petit déjeuner. Quant au déjeuner et au dîner il y a une cantine pour le personnel près de la sortie du parc. On vous fournit aussi votre uniforme: une casquette rouge avec le nom du parc, un tee-shirt jaune et un pantalon noir. Nous fournissons même la crème solaire. Nous commençons la formation demain. Alors: Bonsoir et dormez bien.**

*(3 minutes)*

**(t)    Question number two.**

Your staff meeting continues the following morning.

**You now have one minute to study the question.**

**(f)    Bonjour tout le monde. J'espère que vous avez bien dormi. Aujourd'hui vous allez d'abord vous présenter au groupe pour mieux vous connaître. Ici on parle toujours en français car nous sommes de quinze nationalités différentes. Maintenant je vous explique les règlements du parc. Vous devez toujours arriver à l'heure pour commencer le travail et il est interdit de boire de l'alcool ou de fumer les jours de travail. Cet après-midi vous êtes libres pour explorer le parc. Il fait très beau aujourd'hui et je vous recommande donc d'aller voir notre grande piscine olympique. Ce soir vous pouvez visiter la ville voisine et aller en boîte de nuit ou faire les magasins. Les bus partent de l'entrée du parc toutes les demi-heures jusqu'à une heure du matin.**

*(3 minutes)*

**(t)     Question number three.**

While working in Belgium you meet a colleague, Robert, who comes from Martinique. He tells you a bit about himself, where he has been, and his native country.

**You now have one minute to study the question.**

**(m)     Bonjour, je m'appelle Robert et je viens de la Martinique. L'année prochaine je vais à l'université afin d'étudier les mathématiques. Mais d'abord je fais le tour du monde. J'ai déjà passé trois mois en Australie pour perfectionner mon anglais. Là j'ai travaillé dans une ferme. J'ai beaucoup aimé les animaux bizarres et les gens qui étaient toujours souriants. Ce que je n'aimais pas c'était les insectes dans les salles de bains et les serpents sous les lits! Je suis en Belgique depuis un mois et je la trouve bien différente de la Martinique. D'abord, la Martinique est une île montagneuse. Puis nous mangeons beaucoup plus de fruits et de légumes que les Belges. Tu veux me rendre visite en Martinique? Tu pourrais profiter du beau temps pour bronzer et aussi pour visiter les sites historiques.**

*(3 minutes)*

**(t)     End of test.**

**Now look over your answers.**

*[END OF TRANSCRIPT]*

[BLANK PAGE]

FOR OFFICIAL USE

| | | | | | |
|---|---|---|---|---|---|
| | | | | | |

Mark ☐

# X059/202

NATIONAL
QUALIFICATIONS
2008

WEDNESDAY, 21 MAY
10.30 AM – 11.00 AM

FRENCH
INTERMEDIATE 2
Listening

---

**Fill in these boxes and read what is printed below.**

Full name of centre

_____

Town

_____

Forename(s)

_____

Surname

_____

Date of birth
Day Month Year    Scottish candidate number    Number of seat

When you are told to do so, open your paper.

You will hear three items in French. **Before you hear each item, you will have one minute to study the question.** You will hear each item twice, with an interval of one minute between playings, then you will have time to answer the questions about it before hearing the next item.

Write your answers, **in English**, in this book, in the appropriate spaces.

You may take notes as you are listening to the French, but only in this book.

You may **not** use a French dictionary.

You are not allowed to leave the examination room until the end of the test.

Before leaving the examination room you must give this book to the invigilator. If you do not, you may lose all the marks for this paper.

DO NOT
WRITE IN
THIS
MARGIN

*Points*

1. You have arrived in Belgium to work in an amusement park.

   (*a*) What is the name of the person who is responsible for staff?
   
   Tick **one** box.                                                    1

   | | |
   |---|---|
   | Michelle Dupont | |
   | Michelle Durand | |
   | Michelle Duchamp | |

   (*b*) Why should you contact this person?                            1

   _____

   (*c*) How many hours will you work a week?                           1

   _____

   (*d*) How much will you earn an hour?                                1

   _____

   (*e*) What are you told about the chalet you will share?  Mention any
   **one** thing.                                                       1

   _____

   (*f*) Where is the staff canteen?                                    1

   _____

   (*g*) Describe your uniform.  Mention any **two** things.            2

   _____

   _____

                    *    *    *    *    *

DO NOT
WRITE IN
THIS
MARGIN

*Points*

**2.** Your staff meeting continues the following morning.

(*a*) Why must everyone speak in French?                                                1

_____

(*b*) Which rules must you follow at work?  Mention any **two** things.         2

_____

_____

_____

(*c*) What is suggested you do in the afternoon?  Mention any **one** thing.   1

_____

(*d*) Why might you visit the neighbouring town?  Mention any **one** thing.   1

_____

(*e*) How often do the buses run?                                                        1

_____

*              *              *              *              *

**[Turn over for Question 3 on *Page four***

*Points*

DO NOT
WRITE IN
THIS
MARGIN

3. While working in Belgium you meet a colleague, Robert, who comes from Martinique. He tells you a bit about himself, where he has been, and his native country.

   (*a*)  What is Robert going to study at university?  **1**

   _____

   (*b*)  Why did he go to Australia?  Mention any **one** thing.  **1**

   _____

   (*c*)  What did he like about Australia?  Mention any **one** thing.  **1**

   _____

   (*d*)  What did he not like about Australia?  Mention any **one** thing.  **1**

   _____

   (*e*)  What does he tell you about Martinique?  Mention any **one** thing.  **1**

   _____

   (*f*)  Robert invites you to Martinique.  What does he suggest you can do there?  Mention any **one** thing.  **1**

   _____

*     *     *     *     *

**Total (20  points)
= 20 marks**

[*END OF QUESTION PAPER*]

# X059/204

NATIONAL
QUALIFICATIONS
2008

WEDNESDAY, 21 MAY
11.20 AM – 12.00 NOON

# FRENCH
# INTERMEDIATE 2
Writing

20 marks are allocated to this paper.

You may use a French dictionary.

You are preparing an application for the job advertised below.

| | |
|---|---|
| **Titre du poste:** | Guide touristique |
| **Description de l'offre:** | Guide touristique en France et en Europe de l'Ouest. <br> Hébergement en France. <br> Le/La candidat(e) devra avoir une bonne présentation et le sens des responsabilités. <br> Langues étrangères obligatoires. |

To help you to write your application, you have been given the following checklist of information to give about yourself and to ask about the job:

- name, age, where you live
- leisure interests
- school/college career – subjects studied previously/being studied now
- reasons for application
- request for information about the job.

Make sure you deal with **all** of these points. You could also include the following information:

- any previous links with France or a French-speaking country
- work experience, if any.

You have also been given a way to start and finish this formal type of letter:

**Formal opening to letter of application**

> Monsieur/Madame/Messieurs,
>
> Suite à votre annonce, je me permets de poser ma candidature pour le poste de . . .

**Formal finish to letter of application**

> En espérant que ma demande retiendra votre attention, je vous prie d'accepter, Monsieur/Madame/Messieurs, l'expression de mes sentiments distingués.

Use all of the above to help you write **in French** the letter which should be 120–150 words, excluding the formal phrases you have been given. You may use a French dictionary.

*[END OF QUESTION PAPER]*

# 2009

[BLANK PAGE]

FOR OFFICIAL USE

| | | | | |
|---|---|---|---|---|
| | | | | |

Mark

# X059/201

NATIONAL
QUALIFICATIONS
2009

FRIDAY, 22 MAY
9.00 AM – 10.10 AM

**FRENCH**
INTERMEDIATE 2
Reading

---

**Fill in these boxes and read what is printed below.**

Full name of centre

Town

Forename(s)

Surname

Date of birth
 Day  Month  Year     Scottish candidate number     Number of seat

When you are told to do so, open your paper and write your answers **in English** in the spaces provided.

You may use a French dictionary.

Before leaving the examination room you must give this book to the invigilator. If you do not, you may lose all the marks for this paper.

DO NOT
WRITE IN
THIS
MARGIN

*Points*

1.  On the Internet you read about a competition in which schools can win a place at a European seminar in Strasbourg.

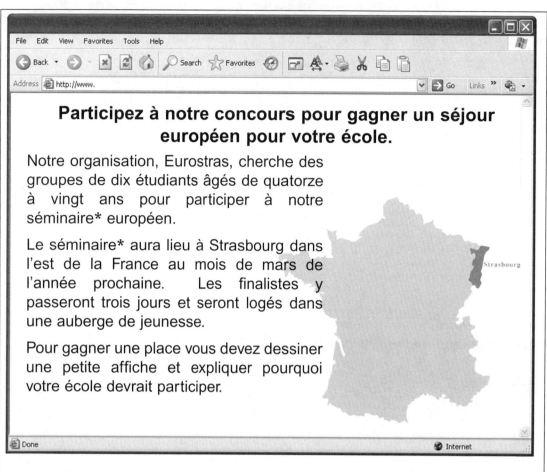

**Participez à notre concours pour gagner un séjour européen pour votre école.**

Notre organisation, Eurostras, cherche des groupes de dix étudiants âgés de quatorze à vingt ans pour participer à notre séminaire* européen.

Le séminaire* aura lieu à Strasbourg dans l'est de la France au mois de mars de l'année prochaine. Les finalistes y passeront trois jours et seront logés dans une auberge de jeunesse.

Pour gagner une place vous devez dessiner une petite affiche et expliquer pourquoi votre école devrait participer.

**\* séminaire = seminar, conference**

(a)  Complete the following sentence.

The Eurostras organisation is looking for students aged between

___14___ and ___26___ .

(b)  When will the seminar take place? Mention any **one** thing.

_Next march_

(c)  Where in Strasbourg will the finalists stay?

_A youth hostle_

(d)  What do you have to do to win a place at the seminar? Mention **two** things.

_Make a poster & say why_
_the school must be chosen_

*Points*

DO NOT
WRITE IN
THIS
MARGIN

**2.** You are very interested in the competition and you read on to find out more.

---

**Premier jour**
Tous les groupes se présentent en français et
rencontrent les autres participants.

**Deuxième jour**
Chaque groupe va en ville pour vendre les produits
traditionnels de son pays. Par exemple de la nourriture, des drapeaux ou
des cartes postales.

**Troisième jour**
Une visite au Parlement, un bâtiment construit en verre, où les groupes
discutent de la politique européenne.

A la fin des trois jours, le groupe qui a le mieux travaillé en équipe gagnera
un prix de 500 Euros.

---

(a) What do the groups do on the first day? Mention any **one** thing. | 1

*They meet the other participants*

(b) Give any **two** examples of traditional products the groups might sell. | 1

*flags & post cards*

(c) On the third day there is a visit to the European Parliament.

   (i) What is the building like? | 1

   *It is built of glass.*

   (ii) What do the groups do during the visit? | 1

   *Meet & talk about European politics*

(d) Which group will win the prize? | 1

*The Group with the most work*

**[Turn over**

DO NOT
WRITE IN
THIS
MARGIN

*Points*

3. You then read an article by Cédric, who was part of last year's winning group. He talks about his time in Strasbourg and what his school did with the money they won.

---

### Mon séjour à Strasbourg

Le séjour à Strasbourg était génial. Pendant mon temps libre je me suis promené dans les rues de la ville et j'ai acheté des cadeaux pour ma famille. Le dernier soir tous les groupes ont fait la fête et nous avons chanté dans toutes les langues. J'étais un peu triste car je devais dire au revoir à mes nouveaux amis.

Notre groupe était content de gagner le prix. Nous avons utilisé l'argent pour créer un jardin dans notre école.

---

(a) What did Cédric do during his free time? Mention **two** things.    2

*He bought presents for his family*
*He took a walk through the city.*

(b) What happened on the last night? Mention any **one** thing.    1

*There was a party*

(c) Why was Cédric a little sad?    1

(d) What did his group do with the prize money?    1

*for creating a garden for the*
*school*

[Turn over for Question 4 on *Pages six, seven* and *eight*

**4.** You read an article in a French magazine.

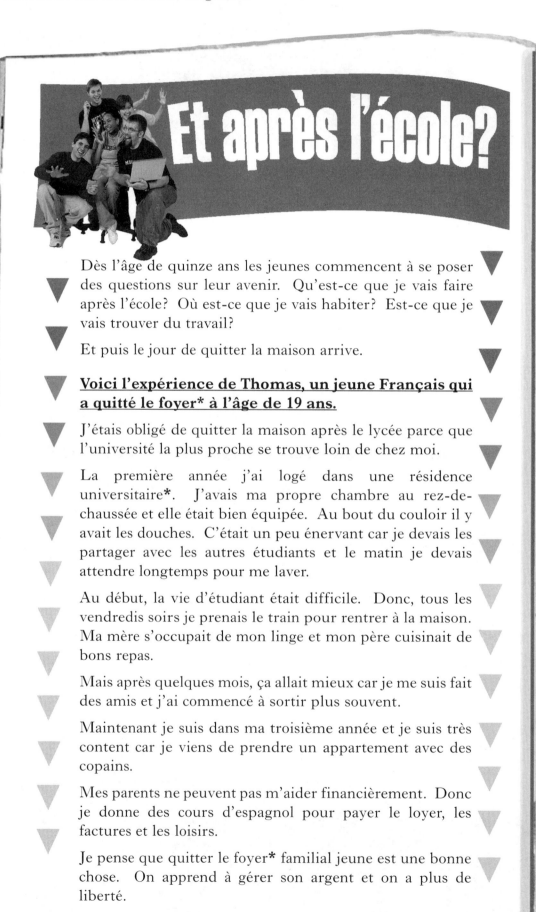

# Et après l'école?

Dès l'âge de quinze ans les jeunes commencent à se poser des questions sur leur avenir. Qu'est-ce que je vais faire après l'école? Où est-ce que je vais habiter? Est-ce que je vais trouver du travail?

Et puis le jour de quitter la maison arrive.

**<u>Voici l'expérience de Thomas, un jeune Français qui a quitté le foyer\* à l'âge de 19 ans.</u>**

J'étais obligé de quitter la maison après le lycée parce que l'université la plus proche se trouve loin de chez moi.

La première année j'ai logé dans une résidence universitaire\*. J'avais ma propre chambre au rez-de-chaussée et elle était bien équipée. Au bout du couloir il y avait les douches. C'était un peu énervant car je devais les partager avec les autres étudiants et le matin je devais attendre longtemps pour me laver.

Au début, la vie d'étudiant était difficile. Donc, tous les vendredis soirs je prenais le train pour rentrer à la maison. Ma mère s'occupait de mon linge et mon père cuisinait de bons repas.

Mais après quelques mois, ça allait mieux car je me suis fait des amis et j'ai commencé à sortir plus souvent.

Maintenant je suis dans ma troisième année et je suis très content car je viens de prendre un appartement avec des copains.

Mes parents ne peuvent pas m'aider financièrement. Donc je donne des cours d'espagnol pour payer le loyer, les factures et les loisirs.

Je pense que quitter le foyer\* familial jeune est une bonne chose. On apprend à gérer son argent et on a plus de liberté.

**4. (continued)**

*Points*

Do not write in this margin

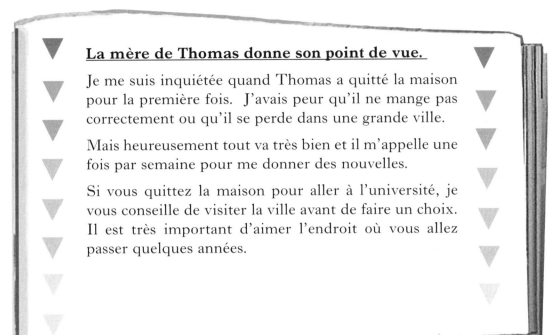

### La mère de Thomas donne son point de vue.

Je me suis inquiétée quand Thomas a quitté la maison pour la première fois. J'avais peur qu'il ne mange pas correctement ou qu'il se perde dans une grande ville.

Mais heureusement tout va très bien et il m'appelle une fois par semaine pour me donner des nouvelles.

Si vous quittez la maison pour aller à l'université, je vous conseille de visiter la ville avant de faire un choix. Il est très important d'aimer l'endroit où vous allez passer quelques années.

\* le foyer                              = the household
\* une résidence universitaire = halls of residence

(a) According to the first paragraph young people ask themselves many questions about their future. Mention any **two**.

    What do i do after School

    Where will i live.

**2**

**Thomas talks about his experience of leaving home to go to university.**

(b) What does Thomas say about his room in the halls of residence? Mention any **two** things.

    His room was well equipped

    His room was on the botton floor

**2**

(c) What annoyed Thomas about the showers? Mention any **one** thing.

**1**

(d) At the beginning he went back home every Friday evening.

    (i) What did his mum do for him?

        Occupied his clothes & washed them

**1**

    (ii) What did his dad do?

        Dad did the meal

**1**

DO NOT
WRITE IN
THIS
MARGIN

Points

4.  **(continued)**

(e)  Why did things get better after a few months?  Mention any **one** thing.    1

He mcall friend)

(f)  Thomas' parents cannot help him financially.

(i)  What does Thomas do to earn money?    1

Get a Job

(ii)  What does he need this money for?  Mention any **two** things.    2

The rent & free-time

(g)  Why does he think it is a good thing to leave home at a young age?
Mention any **one** thing.    1

learn how to look after money

**Thomas' mother gives her point of view.**

(h)  What was Thomas' mother worried about when he left home?
Mention any **one** thing.    1

He would not eat properly

(i)  How does she know everything is fine?  Mention **one** thing.    1

(j)  Why does she advise young people to visit the town before choosing a
university?    1

25/30    A+

Total (30 points)

= 30 marks

*[END OF QUESTION PAPER]*

# X059/203

NATIONAL
QUALIFICATIONS
2009

FRIDAY, 22 MAY
10.30 AM – 11.00 AM
(APPROX)

# FRENCH
## INTERMEDIATE 2
Listening Transcript

**This paper must not be seen by any candidate.**

The material overleaf is provided for use in an emergency only (eg the recording or equipment proving faulty) or where permission has been given in advance by SQA for the material to be read to candidates with additional support needs. The material must be read exactly as printed.

## Transcript—Intermediate 2

**Instructions to reader(s):**

For each item, read the English **once**, then read the French **twice**, with an interval of 1 minute between the two readings. On completion of the second reading, pause for the length of time indicated in brackets after each item, to allow the candidates to write their answers.

Where special arrangements have been agreed in advance to allow the reading of the material, those sections marked **(f)** should be read by a female speaker and those marked **(m)** by a male: those sections marked **(t)** should be read by the teacher.

**(t)**  You are attending a European seminar in Strasbourg.

**Question number one.**

Nadine, one of the other participants, tells you about her school.

**You now have one minute to study the question.**

**(f)**  Je fréquente un grand lycée international au centre de Genève en Suisse. Comme les élèves sont de toutes nationalités, les cours se font en anglais, sauf les cours de langues bien sûr. Moi, j'apprends l'allemand en langue étrangère. Je la trouve un peu difficile et en plus le prof est très ennuyeux. Je fais 7 matières au total mais ma matière préférée est le dessin. Je l'aime bien car ça m'aide à me détendre et à oublier mes problèmes. De plus je fais des dessins pour notre magazine scolaire qui paraît chaque trimestre. On y trouve aussi des articles sur les problèmes familiaux ou des conseils pour avoir de meilleures notes à l'école. Le magazine est vendu aux élèves, aux profs, aux parents et aux habitants de notre ville. Le magazine a un grand succès et fait un bon profit. On donne un peu de l'argent des ventes à une association qui aide les enfants pauvres.

*(3 minutes)*

**(t)**  **Question number two.**

Nadine then goes on to tell you about her holiday in Greece last year.

**You now have one minute to study the question.**

**(f)**  L'année dernière je suis partie avec mes amis pour quinze jours en Grèce. C'était la première fois que j'allais en vacances sans mes parents et j'étais à la fois excitée mais aussi un peu anxieuse. J'avais raison de l'être. Les problèmes ont commencé à l'aéroport. D'abord un de mes amis avait oublié son passeport. Ensuite l'avion avait 5 heures de retard à cause du brouillard. Quand on est enfin arrivé en Grèce, on a pris un taxi pour aller à notre villa. Elle était très sale et il n'y avait pas de frigo. Le reste de la première semaine s'est passé sans trop de problèmes. Il a fait super beau et on passait les journées à se baigner dans la piscine et à jouer aux cartes sur la terrasse. Et puis un jour on a décidé de louer des vélos. Quelle mauvaise idée! Moi, je suis tombée de vélo et je me suis cassé la jambe. On a été obligé de m'emmener à l'hôpital et c'est là-bas que j'ai passé le reste de mes vacances. C'était vraiment des vacances désastreuses.

*(3 minutes)*

**(t)** **Question number three.**

While you are in Strasbourg, you listen to the radio. You hear a news item about a break-in at a big supermarket.

**You now have one minute to study the question.**

**(m)** Un grand hypermarché a été cambriolé cette nuit à trois heures du matin. L'hypermarché se trouve à 8 km de Strasbourg et est un des plus grands de la ville. Les 3 voleurs ont pris des vêtements, des ordinateurs et de l'alcool. La police croit que ces jeunes hommes doivent connaître quelqu'un qui travaille dans le magasin parce qu'ils sont entrés sans déclencher l'alarme. Ils ont été filmés par des caméras de surveillance et ont entre 18 et 24 ans. Ils sont tous de taille moyenne et étaient habillés en jean et pull noir avec des baskets blanches. Un des voleurs a les cheveux longs et blonds et porte des lunettes. Les 3 voleurs sont partis par le parking du sous-sol dans un camion vert. Ni le camion ni les voleurs n'ont été retrouvés. La police cherche des témoins. Si vous avez des informations veuillez appeler le 03-88-20-54-16.

*(3 minutes)*

**(t)** **End of test.**

**Now look over your answers.**

*[END OF TRANSCRIPT]*

[BLANK PAGE]

FOR OFFICIAL USE

Mark ☐

# X059/202

NATIONAL
QUALIFICATIONS
2009

FRIDAY, 22 MAY
10.30 AM – 11.00 AM
(APPROX)

## FRENCH
## INTERMEDIATE 2
Listening

---

**Fill in these boxes and read what is printed below.**

Full name of centre

Town

Forename(s)

Surname

Date of birth
Day  Month  Year     Scottish candidate number     Number of seat

When you are told to do so, open your paper.

You will hear three items in French. **Before you hear each item, you will have one minute to study the question.** You will hear each item twice, with an interval of one minute between playings, then you will have time to answer the questions about it before hearing the next item.

Write your answers, **in English**, in this book, in the appropriate spaces.

You may take notes as you are listening to the French, but only in this book.

You may **not** use a French dictionary.

You are not allowed to leave the examination room until the end of the test.

Before leaving the examination room you must give this book to the invigilator. If you do not, you may lose all the marks for this paper.

*Points*

You are attending a European seminar in Strasbourg.

1. Nadine, one of the other participants, tells you about her school.

   (a) Where is Nadine's school?  Mention any **one** thing.          1

   _In  Switzerland_

   (b) Mention **two** things she says about learning German.          2

   _It is difficult_

   _And the teacher is boring_

   (c) Why is art Nadine's favourite subject?  Mention **two** things.          2

   _Art & design_

   (d) There is a magazine in her school.  What are the articles about?
   Mention any **one** thing.          1

   _Family problems_

   (e) Who do they help with the money they make from the magazine?          1

   _Association for Poor Children_

   \*     \*     \*     \*     \*

DO NOT
WRITE IN
THIS
MARGIN

*Points*

2.  Nadine then goes on to tell you about her holiday in Greece last year.

(a)  How long did Nadine go on holiday for?                              1

_____15 days_____

(b)  Their problems started at the airport.

(i)  What was the first problem they had?                           1

_____They forget Passports_____

(ii)  Why was the plane late?                                       1

_____

(c)  What problems did they have with their villa? Mention any **one** thing.   1

_____

(d)  The rest of the week went well. What did they do during the day?
Mention any **one** thing.                                              1

_____S Very beautiful & went Swimming____

(e)  They decided to hire bikes. Why was this a bad idea? Mention any
**two** things.                                                         2

_____She broke her leg & can't____

_____ride a bike._____

\*    \*    \*    \*    \*

**[Turn over for Question 3 on *Page four***

DO NOT
WRITE IN
THIS
MARGIN

*Points*

3. While you are in Strasbourg, you listen to the radio. You hear a news item about a break-in at a big supermarket.

(a) At what time did the break-in take place?    **1**

_____ 3:00 am _____

(b) What did the thieves steal? Mention any **two** things.    **2**

_____ A computer _____

_____ alcohol _____

(c) What were the thieves wearing? Complete the following sentence.    **1**

They were wearing jeans, a black ___ jumper ___ and

___ White ___ trainers.

(d) How did they escape? Mention any **one** thing.    **1**

_____ a green van _____

(e) Complete the telephone number you should call if you have any information.    **1**

03–88–20– 55 – 07

\*     \*     \*     \*     \*

Total (20 points)
= 20 marks

*[END OF QUESTION PAPER]*

$\dfrac{16}{20}$  (–A)

# X059/204

NATIONAL
QUALIFICATIONS
2009

FRIDAY, 22 MAY
11.20 AM – 12.00 NOON

FRENCH
INTERMEDIATE 2
Writing

20 marks are allocated to this paper.

You may use a French dictionary.

You are preparing an application for the job advertised below.

| | |
|---|---|
| **Employeur:** | **Hôtel IBIS – Strasbourg** |
| **Poste:** | Serveur/serveuse |
| **Profil:** | Responsable du service dans le restaurant de l'hôtel. Vous devez parler l'anglais et le français. |
| **Renseignements:** | Pour plus de détails sur les horaires, le salaire, l'hébergement etc. **Contactez** Hôtel IBIS **19, Place de la Cathédrale** **67000 Strasbourg, France** |

To help you to write your application, you have been given the following checklist of information to give about yourself and to ask about the job. Make sure you deal with **all** of these points:

- name, age, where you live
- leisure interests
- school/college career – subjects studied previously/being studied now
- reasons for application
- request for information about the job.

You could also include the following information:

- any previous links with France or a French-speaking country
- work experience, if any.

You have also been given a way to start and finish this formal type of letter:

**Formal opening to letter of application**

Monsieur/Madame/Messieurs,

Suite à votre annonce, je me permets de poser ma candidature pour le poste de . . .

**Formal finish to letter of application**

En espérant que ma demande retiendra votre attention, je vous prie d'accepter, Monsieur/Madame/Messieurs, l'expression de mes sentiments distingués.

Use all of the above to help you write **in French** the letter which should be 120–150 words, excluding the formal phrases you have been given. You may use a French dictionary.

*[END OF QUESTION PAPER]*

# 2010

[BLANK PAGE]

FOR OFFICIAL USE

|  |  |  |  |  |  |
|--|--|--|--|--|--|
|  |  |  |  |  |  |

Mark ☐

# X059/201

NATIONAL
QUALIFICATIONS
2010

TUESDAY, 18 MAY
9.00 AM – 10.10 AM

**FRENCH**
**INTERMEDIATE 2**
Reading

---

**Fill in these boxes and read what is printed below.**

Full name of centre

Town

Forename(s)

Surname

Date of birth

Day    Month    Year      Scottish candidate number      Number of seat

When you are told to do so, open your paper and write your answers **in English** in the spaces provided.

You may use a French dictionary.

Before leaving the examination room you must give this book to the Invigilator. If you do not, you may lose all the marks for this paper.

DO NOT
WRITE IN
THIS
MARGIN

*Marks*

1. You want to take a year out to work in France. You see an advert on the Internet from a Senegalese family looking for an au pair to help look after their children.

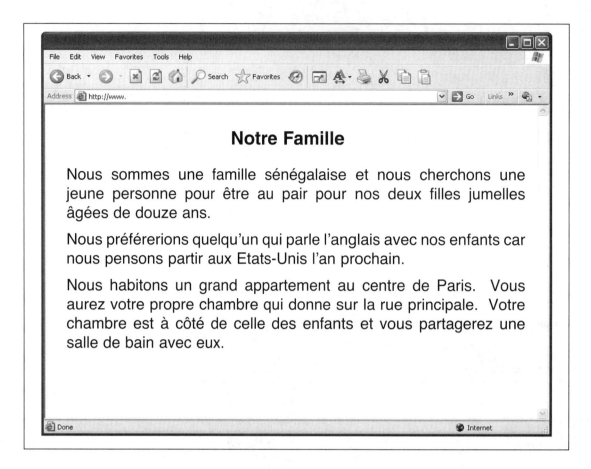

**Notre Famille**

Nous sommes une famille sénégalaise et nous cherchons une jeune personne pour être au pair pour nos deux filles jumelles âgées de douze ans.

Nous préférerions quelqu'un qui parle l'anglais avec nos enfants car nous pensons partir aux Etats-Unis l'an prochain.

Nous habitons un grand appartement au centre de Paris. Vous aurez votre propre chambre qui donne sur la rue principale. Votre chambre est à côté de celle des enfants et vous partagerez une salle de bain avec eux.

(*a*) Mention **two** things about the two girls in the family.    (2)

_They are from Senegal ✓_

_They are both 17 years old ✓_

(*b*) Why would the family prefer someone who speaks English?    (1)

_Because they need to practise english because they are going to the USA._

(*c*) What are you told about your living arrangements? Tick (✓) the **two** correct sentences.    (2) (1)

| | |
|---|---|
| Your bedroom must be kept clean. | |
| You will have the main bedroom. | |
| Your bedroom is next to the children's. | |
| You will have to share the bathroom. | |

*Marks*

2. You are interested and you read on to find out more about the job.

---

**Le travail**

Vous travaillerez tous les jours sauf le mercredi et le dimanche.

Vous aiderez les enfants à faire leurs devoirs et vous vous occuperez d'eux le soir si nous sortons.

Vous ferez de petits travaux ménagers comme le repassage ou aider à la préparation des repas.

Pendant vos jours de congé, vous pourrez suivre des cours de français ou aller vous promener dans les quartiers voisins.

---

(*a*) When will you have to work? ⓵

on Wednesdays & Sundays

(*b*) What will you have to do for the children? ⓶

Help with eating & homework & look after the kids

(*c*) What household tasks will you be expected to carry out? Mention any **one**. ⓵

Help with preparing dinner

(*d*) What does the family suggest you could do on your days off? Mention any **one** thing. ⓵

Take a course in french

**[Turn over**

DO NOT
WRITE IN
THIS
MARGIN

*Marks*

3. You have been successful in your application for the job. While in France the family shows you an article about Senegal, their home country, which is in West Africa.

Le Sénégal était une colonie française et l'influence française y est vraiment sentie: la langue française est parlée partout et il existe encore des bâtiments historiques qui datent de cette époque là.

Le tourisme au Sénégal continue d'augmenter grâce au soleil qui brille pratiquement toute l'année et à l'accueil chaleureux de sa population. Le Sénégal offre beaucoup de choses aux touristes comme, par exemple, des côtes de toute beauté, des villages traditionnels de pêcheurs et des villes animées.

(a) Senegal was a French colony. How is the French influence still felt in Senegal?

*2*

The main language is french & there are french historical castles.

(b) Why is tourism continuing to increase in Senegal? Mention any **one** thing.

*1*

Because of the beautiful sunshine X

(c) What does Senegal have to offer to tourists? Mention any **two** things.

*2*

traditional village & beautiful landscapes

**[Turn over for Question 4 on *Pages six, seven* and *eight***

**4.** You read an article in a magazine about holidays.

## Les vacances arrivent!

Tout le monde a besoin de vacances pour oublier le travail ou les études et pour s'échapper de la vie quotidienne. Mais où faut-il aller pour passer des vacances idéales?

Deux personnes nous parlent de leurs vacances bien différentes.

### Caroline

L'année dernière était une année très difficile pour moi. J'ai rompu avec mon copain puis j'ai été malade pendant quelques mois. J'ai donc décidé de partir une semaine en Espagne. Je ne voulais que me reposer en faisant un peu de lecture et de bronzage.

Le premier jour, j'ai décidé d'aller à la plage, mais quel désastre! Il y avait trop de monde, pas assez de place pour poser ma serviette et en plus, comme il faisait très chaud, j'ai pris un coup de soleil très douloureux.

Les soirées n'étaient pas mieux. La nourriture dans l'hôtel n'était pas bonne et je n'arrivais pas à dormir à cause du bruit des boîtes de nuit. De plus, il y avait des moustiques qui me piquaient sans cesse.

A la fin de la semaine je me sentais encore plus fatiguée et en fait, j'avais besoin de vacances en rentrant à la maison!

### La famille Casse

Avant, notre famille n'aimait pas partir en vacances parce qu'on avait toujours peur de laisser la maison vide et il n'y avait personne pour arroser le jardin ou les fleurs. Mais un jour, on a lu un article dans un magazine qu'il était possible de faire un échange de maison. On s'est tout de suite renseigné et maintenant on part en vacances chaque année chez des gens, qui eux, viennent chez nous. C'est idéal pour notre famille. On a tout le confort d'une maison et on est loin des touristes. On fait aussi la connaissance des autres familles qui vivent dans les alentours et donc nos deux enfants ne s'ennuient jamais.

De plus, ces vacances ne sont pas chères car il n'y a qu'un billet d'avion et quelques frais d'agences à payer. Le seul inconvénient est qu'on doit faire le ménage avant de partir!

DO NOT
WRITE IN
THIS
MARGIN

*Marks*

4. **(continued)**

(a) Why does everyone need a holiday? Mention any **one** thing.    1

_To escape from everything Wj_

**Caroline**

(b) Why had it been a difficult year for Caroline? Mention any **one** thing.   1

_She has been very sick_

(c) Where and for how long did she go on holiday?   1

_She went to Spain for a week_

(d) What did she want to do on holiday? Mention any **two** things.   2

_Relaxation et récipe books_

(e) Why was her first day at the beach a disaster? Mention any **two** things.   2

_It was too hot & She got Sunburn_

(f) What problems did she have in the evenings? Mention any **two** things.   2

_There were mosquitoes & the noises at night_

DO NOT
WRITE IN
THIS
MARGIN

*Marks*

4. **(continued)**

**La famille Casse**

(g) Why did the Casse family not like going on holiday? Mention any **one** thing.

<u>Nobody left to water the flower</u>

1

(h) How did they find out about the possibility of doing a house exchange?

<u>From an article in a magazine</u>

1

(i) Why is this type of holiday ideal for the Casse family? Mention any **three** things.

<u>The get the usual comforts of</u>
<u>a home, Away from tourist, the</u>
<u>children will never get bored</u>

3

(j) Why is this type of holiday not expensive? Mention any **one** thing.

<u>They don't need to pay for transport</u>

1

$\frac{25}{30}$    (A)    **Total (30)**

83%

*[END OF QUESTION PAPER]*

# X059/203

NATIONAL
QUALIFICATIONS
2010

TUESDAY, 18 MAY
10.30 AM – 11.00 AM
(APPROX)

**FRENCH
INTERMEDIATE 2**
Listening Transcript

**This paper must not be seen by any candidate.**

The material overleaf is provided for use in an emergency only (eg the recording or equipment proving faulty) or where permission has been given in advance by SQA for the material to be read to candidates with additional support needs. The material must be read exactly as printed.

Transcript—Intermediate 2

---

**Instructions to reader(s):**

For each item, read the English **once**, then read the French **twice**, with an interval of 1 minute between the two readings. On completion of the second reading, pause for the length of time indicated in brackets after each item, to allow the candidates to write their answers.

Where special arrangements have been agreed in advance to allow the reading of the material, those sections marked **(f)** should be read by a female speaker and those marked **(m)** by a male: those sections marked **(t)** should be read by the teacher.

---

**(t)**  You are working as an au pair for a family in France. One evening the family invites friends, Pauline and Bruno, to dinner.

**Question number one.**

Pauline tells you about a school trip she went on to England.

**You now have one minute to study the question.**

**(f)**  Quand j'avais 16 ans j'ai participé à un échange scolaire avec mon école. Nous avons passé un mois dans le sud de l'Angleterre avec une famille d'accueil. La famille était vraiment gentille et je me suis très bien entendue avec leur fille, Louise. Elle avait le même âge que moi et on avait les mêmes intérêts, surtout la mode. Tous les matins, j'allais à l'école avec Louise. Les cours de français étaient marrants. Le prof m'a demandé de parler en français de ma famille et de ma ville, c'était vraiment très intéressant. J'ai trouvé l'école très différente de mon lycée. En Grande-Bretagne, les profs sont plus compréhensifs et les élèves ont moins de devoirs. Je passais les soirées avec ma famille d'accueil et après le dîner, on jouait aux cartes ou on discutait des différences entre la France et l'Angleterre. J'ai vraiment adoré l'Angleterre et après ce séjour j'ai décidé d'étudier les langues étrangères.

*(3 minutes)*

**(t)**  **Question number two.**

Pauline goes on to tell you about the gap year she took after leaving school.

**You now have one minute to study the question.**

**(f)**  Après le lycée et avant de commencer à faire de longues études à la fac, j'ai décidé de prendre une année sabbatique et de voyager en Europe. Au début mes parents étaient contre parce qu'ils croyaient que j'étais trop jeune et qu'il était trop dangereux pour une jeune fille de voyager seule. Heureusement, ma tante qui vivait au Portugal a dit que je pourrais loger chez elle pendant quelque temps. Mes parents ont donc accepté à condition que je les contacte tous les jours et que j'aide ma tante à faire les tâches ménagères. Malheureusement, je me suis mal entendue avec ma tante. Je devais rentrer à 21 heures tous les soirs et je n'avais pas le droit d'inviter mes copains à la maison. Par conséquent, j'ai décidé de louer un appartement avec mes nouveaux amis. Pour payer le logement j'ai trouvé un petit boulot à la plage où je vendais des glaces. J'ai fini par passer toute l'année au Portugal. D'accord, je n'ai peut-être pas fait le tour de l'Europe mais j'ai eu ma première expérience de la vie sans mes parents et j'ai gagné beaucoup de confiance en moi.

*(3 minutes)*

**(t)** **Question number three.**

Bruno talks about the voluntary work he did in Senegal, a country in Africa.

**You now have one minute to study the question.**

**(m)** Moi aussi, j'ai travaillé à l'étranger. Je suis parti au Sénégal il y a un an pour participer à un projet de volontariat qui a duré 6 semaines. Mon projet était de travailler dans une école maternelle avec des enfants âgés de trois à six ans. Les enfants étaient fascinés par ma vie et je devais répondre à toutes leurs questions sur la France et l'Europe. Je devais aussi organiser toutes sortes d'activités pour stimuler l'intérêt des jeunes enfants, par exemple des jeux et des chansons. Les gens du Sénégal sont extraordinaires. Ils ont peu d'argent, donc en général ils sont très pauvres et pourtant ils sont toujours très souriants. Ce projet a vraiment changé ma vie. Depuis mon retour en France, je pense continuellement aux Sénégalais que j'ai rencontrés là-bas et j'ai déjà l'intention de repartir en fin d'année pour les retrouver. A mon avis, c'est en participant à un tel projet que l'on apprend vraiment à connaître un pays et ses habitants.

*(3 minutes)*

**(t)** **End of test.**

**Now look over your answers.**

*[END OF TRANSCRIPT]*

[BLANK PAGE]

FOR OFFICIAL USE

| | | | | | |
|---|---|---|---|---|---|

# X059/202

Mark

NATIONAL
QUALIFICATIONS
2010

TUESDAY, 18 MAY
10.30 AM – 11.00 AM
(APPROX)

**FRENCH**
**INTERMEDIATE 2**
Listening

---

**Fill in these boxes and read what is printed below.**

Full name of centre

Town

Forename(s)

Surname

Date of birth

Day    Month    Year        Scottish candidate number        Number of seat

When you are told to do so, open your paper.

You will hear three items in French. **Before you hear each item, you will have one minute to study the question.** You will hear each item twice, with an interval of one minute between playings, then you will have time to answer the questions about it before hearing the next item.

Write your answers, **in English**, in this book, in the appropriate spaces.

You may take notes as you are listening to the French, but only in this book.

You may **not** use a French dictionary.

You are not allowed to leave the examination room until the end of the test.

Before leaving the examination room you must give this book to the Invigilator. If you do not, you may lose all the marks for this paper.

DO NOT
WRITE IN
THIS
MARGIN

*Marks*

You are working as an au pair for a family in France. One evening the family invites friends, Pauline and Bruno, to dinner.

1.  Pauline tells you about a school trip she went on to England.

    (*a*)  How old was Pauline when she went on the school trip?   **1**

    16 years old

    (*b*)  Why did Pauline and Louise get on well?   **2**

    She went to school

    (*c*)  What did the French teacher ask her to talk about? Mention **two** things.   **1**

    About her town & family

    (*d*)  Pauline compares her school with those in Great Britain. What did she find different in British schools? Mention any **one** thing.   **1**

    There is more homework in france

    (*e*)  How did Pauline spend the evenings with the family after dinner? Mention any **one** thing.   **1**

    They played cards together

    (*f*)  What did Pauline decide to do after her trip to England?

    travel there again

    \*    \*    \*    \*    \*

*Marks*

2. Pauline goes on to tell you about the gap year she took after leaving school.

   (a) Why were her parents against her taking a gap year? Mention any **one** thing.

   _She was too young_

   **1**

   (b) Pauline's aunt in Portugal offered to let Pauline stay. On what conditions was she allowed to stay with her aunt? Mention any **one**.

   _That she stayed in touch with them_

   **1**

   (c) Unfortunately, Pauline did not get on with her aunt.

   (i) Mention any **one** reason she gives for this.

   _She was not allowed to bring friends to the house._

   **1**

   (ii) What happened as a result of these problems?

   _She stayed in a flat_

   **1**

   (d) What job did Pauline find in Portugal?

   _She worked on the beach_

   **1**

   (e) What did Pauline gain from her year in Portugal? Mention any **one** thing.

   **1**

   * * * * *

**[Turn over for Question 3 on *Page four***

DO NOT
WRITE IN
THIS
MARGIN

*Marks*

**3.** Bruno talks about the voluntary work he did in Senegal, a country in Africa.

(*a*) When did Bruno go to Senegal?

_A years age_

1

(*b*) What did the project involve?  Complete the sentence.

He worked in a __school__ with children between __3__

and __16__ years old.

2

(*c*) Mention any **one** activity Bruno had to organise.

_Sports games_

1

(*d*) Why did he find the people of Senegal extraordinary?

_They are so poor but still_

_happy_

2

(*e*) What does Bruno say you learn by taking part in such a project?

1

\*    \*    \*    \*    \*

75%    15/20    (-A)    **Total (20)**

*[END OF QUESTION PAPER]*

# X059/204

NATIONAL
QUALIFICATIONS
2010

TUESDAY, 18 MAY
11.20 AM – 12.00 NOON

# FRENCH
## INTERMEDIATE 2
Writing

20 marks are allocated to this paper.

You may use a French dictionary.

You are preparing an application for the job advertised below.

| | |
|---|---|
| **Poste:** | Aide de bureau.  Nous recherchons une personne responsable pour |
| | • répondre au téléphone |
| | • classer des documents |
| **Profil:** | Il faut avoir de bonnes aptitudes d'organisation, la connaissance d'une langue étrangère et être capable de bien travailler avec les autres. |
| **Renseignements:** | Pour plus de détails sur les horaires, le salaire etc. contactez: |

**Madame TEMMIN**
Agence Auban
25 rue du Taur
Toulouse
31000 France

To help you to write your application, you have been given the following checklist of information to give about yourself and to ask about the job.  Make sure you deal with **all** of these points:

- name, age, where you live
- leisure interests
- school/college career – subjects studied previously/being studied now
- reasons for application
- request for information about the job.

You could also include the following information:
- any previous links with France or a French-speaking country
- work experience, if any.

You have also been given a way to start and finish this formal type of letter:

**Formal opening to letter of application**

Monsieur/Madame/Messieurs,

Suite à votre annonce, je me permets de poser ma candidature pour le poste de . . .

**Formal finish to letter of application**

En espérant que ma demande retiendra votre attention, je vous prie d'accepter, Monsieur/Madame/Messieurs, l'expression de mes sentiments distingués.

Use all of the above to help you write **in French** the letter which should be 120–150 words, excluding the formal phrases you have been given.  You may use a French dictionary.

[END OF QUESTION PAPER]

[BLANK PAGE]

FOR OFFICIAL USE

Mark

# X059/201

NATIONAL
QUALIFICATIONS
2011

TUESDAY, 17 MAY
9.00 AM – 10.10 AM

FRENCH
INTERMEDIATE 2
Reading

---

**Fill in these boxes and read what is printed below.**

Full name of centre

Town

Forename(s)

Surname

Date of birth

Day    Month    Year       Scottish candidate number         Number of seat

When you are told to do so, open your paper and write your answers **in English** in the spaces provided.

You may use a French dictionary.

Before leaving the examination room you must give this book to the Invigilator. If you do not, you may lose all the marks for this paper.

DO NOT
WRITE IN
THIS
MARGIN

*Marks*

1. You read this advertisement on the Internet about learning French in a language school in Montpellier.

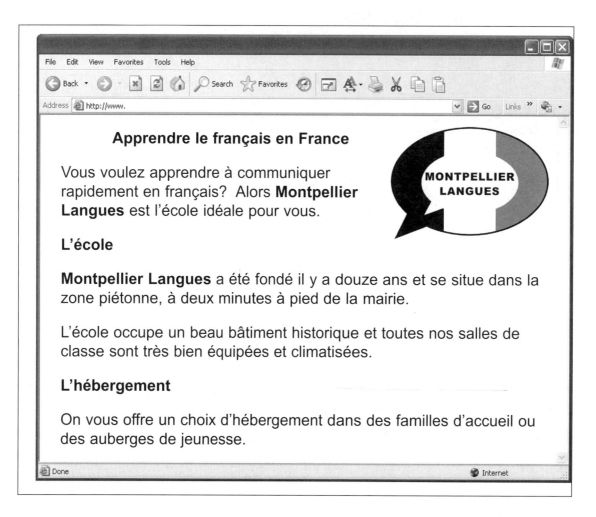

### Apprendre le français en France

Vous voulez apprendre à communiquer rapidement en français? Alors **Montpellier Langues** est l'école idéale pour vous.

### L'école

**Montpellier Langues** a été fondé il y a douze ans et se situe dans la zone piétonne, à deux minutes à pied de la mairie.

L'école occupe un beau bâtiment historique et toutes nos salles de classe sont très bien équipées et climatisées.

### L'hébergement

On vous offre un choix d'hébergement dans des familles d'accueil ou des auberges de jeunesse.

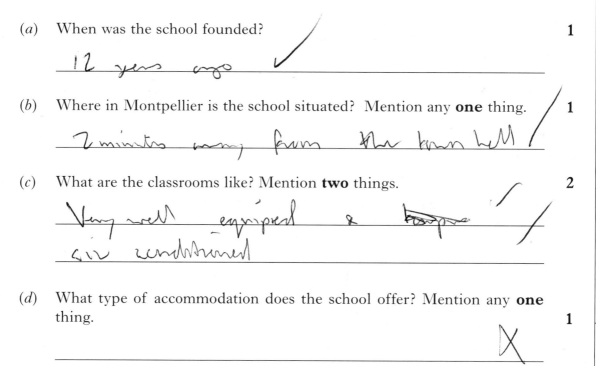

(a) When was the school founded?

12 years ago

1

(b) Where in Montpellier is the school situated? Mention any **one** thing.

2 minutes away from the town hall

1

(c) What are the classrooms like? Mention **two** things.

Very well equiped & air conditioned

2

(d) What type of accommodation does the school offer? Mention any **one** thing.

1

*Marks*

**2.** You are interested and you read on to find out more about the lessons.

---

### PROGRAMME DES COURS

**Les cours**

Les cours ont lieu tout au long de l'année sauf les jours fériés et ils commencent toujours le lundi. Ils se font en petits groupes et pendant les cours du matin les étudiants travailleront l'écoute, la lecture et l'écrit.

L'après-midi les étudiants auront l'occasion de pratiquer la langue dans des situations réelles, par exemple: appeler la gare SNCF pour se renseigner sur les horaires, acheter des produits frais au marché, prendre rendez-vous chez le médecin etc.

---

(*a*) Complete the sentence.                                                      1

Lessons take place all year except _____ monday X _____.

(*b*) What will the students work on during the morning lessons? Mention
any **two** things.                                                               2

listening & writing

(*c*) In the afternoons, the students will have the opportunity to practise their
French in real life situations. Give any **two** examples.                        2

Buy products from the super market
and call SNCF about train times

**[Turn over**

*Marks*

3. You read an article in a French magazine about the summer holidays.

---

**Les vacances scolaires, sont-elles pour se reposer?**

A la fin de l'année scolaire, il est souvent très difficile de s'adapter aux vacances. Il est important que les élèves prennent le temps de se détendre, et de voir des copains.

Mais en réalité beaucoup de jeunes continuent à étudier pendant les vacances, surtout ceux qui ont été malades pendant l'année scolaire.

D'autres gagnent de l'argent en tondant les gazons et en promenant les chiens des voisins pour s'acheter un nouvel ordinateur ou se payer des vacances à l'étranger.

---

(a) What is it important for pupils to do once they are on holiday? Mention any **one** thing.    1

to socialise with friends ✓

(b) Why do some pupils continue to study during the holidays?    1

So that they are prepared for the X next school year.

(c) What do some young people do to earn money?    2

They get paid to walk dogs & mow the grass

(d) What do they do with the money they earn? Mention any **one** thing.    1

Save it for the holiday or X

**[Turn over for Question 4 on *Pages six, seven* and *eight***

**4.** You then find an article about relationships between grandparents and grandchildren.

## Les grands-parents! Ça passe ou ça casse?

Lorsqu'on est petit, on adore aller chez ses grands-parents pour passer une journée au bord d'un lac et jeter du pain aux canards. Mais en grandissant on préfère sortir en boîte avec des copains plutôt que de jouer aux jeux de société avec des personnes âgées.

### Sandrine nous parle de ses relations avec ses grands-parents.

Quand j'étais petite, je voyais mes grands-parents tous les mardis soirs car je n'avais pas d'école le mercredi. Je m'amusais bien chez eux. Ils vivent près de la mer, alors le matin on faisait des châteaux de sable et le soir ils me lisaient une histoire pour m'endormir.

Mais les choses ont changé dès que je suis entrée au lycée. Ma grand-mère a commencé à me critiquer tout le temps. Elle n'aime pas la façon dont je m'habille, les bijoux que je mets et elle dit que je suis trop jeune pour porter du maquillage. Quant à mon grand-père, il me traite comme si j'avais toujours huit ans.

Mes parents et moi leur rendons visite une fois par semaine et nous passons les fêtes ensemble mais ce n'est pas comme avant. J'espère qu'en vieillissant je me rapprocherai d'eux à nouveau.

### Marcel nous parle de ses relations avec ses petits-enfants.

J'ai soixante-douze ans et j'ai perdu ma femme il y a cinq ans. Heureusement, j'ai deux filles et quatre petits-enfants merveilleux. Ils me rendent visite au moins trois fois par semaine et ils m'aident avec le ménage et le jardin.

Sophie, ma petite-fille de onze ans, m'apprend à utiliser mon ordinateur. Grâce à son aide, je peux faire mes courses sur Internet et aussi communiquer avec mon neveu qui habite aux Etats-Unis.

Quand j'étais jeune, mes grands-parents étaient plutôt strictes. Par exemple, à table je devais me tenir droit sur ma chaise et ne jamais interrompre les conversations. De plus, je n'aurais jamais osé leur parler de mes goûts musicaux.

Moi au contraire, je suis beaucoup plus détendu avec mes petits-enfants. J'adore parler des choses qui les intéressent et leur donner des conseils quand ils ont des problèmes. Vivent les jeunes!

*Marks*

**4. (continued)**

(a) According to the article we love going to our grandparents when we are young. What do we like doing with them? Mention any **one** thing.    1

*She goes to the lake to feed the birds*

**Sandrine speaks about her relationship with her grandparents.**

(b) Why did Sandrine go to her grandparents on Tuesday evenings?    1

*Because there is no school on wednesdays*

(c) (i) What did they do together in the morning?    1

*The made lots of sand castles*

(ii) What did her grandparents do in the evening?    1

*? X*

(d) Sandrine says things have changed.

(i) Why does her grandmother criticise her now? Mention any **two** things.    2

*He thinks she is far too young to wear make-up & totals jewllery*

(ii) How does her grandfather treat her?    1

*?*

(e) What does she hope will happen when she gets older?    1

*That thing will become closer*

**Marcel speaks about his relationship with his grandchildren.**

(f) What do his grandchildren help him with? Mention **two** things.    1

*Doing the housework & gardening*

[turn over to page eight for questions 4(g) to 4(i)

DO NOT
WRITE IN
THIS
MARGIN

*Marks*

4. **(continued)**

(*g*)  He speaks about his granddaughter Sophie.

(i)  What does she do for him?    1

Helps him with the computer ✓

(ii)  Thanks to her help, what can he do now?    2

He can surf the internet & contact his relatives in the US    1

(*h*)  Marcel says that his grandparents were strict.  Mention any **two** examples he gives to show this.    2

He was told not to interrupt conversation & sit up straight

(*i*)  What examples does he give to show that he is more relaxed with his grandchildren?  Mention any **one** thing.    1

?                    ✗

22 / 30    B+    **Total (30)**

*[END OF QUESTION PAPER]*

# X059/203

NATIONAL
QUALIFICATIONS
2011

TUESDAY, 17 MAY
10.30 AM – 11.00 AM
(APPROX)

FRENCH
INTERMEDIATE 2
Listening Transcript

**This paper must not be seen by any candidate.**

The material overleaf is provided for use in an emergency only (eg the recording or equipment proving faulty) or where permission has been given in advance by SQA for the material to be read to candidates with additional support needs. The material must be read exactly as printed.

## Transcript—Intermediate 2

> **Instructions to reader(s):**
>
> For each item, read the English **once**, then read the French **three times**, with an interval of 1 minute between the three readings. On completion of the third reading, pause for the length of time indicated in brackets after each item, to allow the candidates to write their answers.
>
> Where special arrangements have been agreed in advance to allow the reading of the material, those sections marked **(f)** should be read by a female speaker and those marked **(m)** by a male; those sections marked **(t)** should be read by the teacher.

**(t)** While in France, you are listening to the radio.

**Question number one.**

You hear a talk by Jérôme, whose class has helped Harona, who lives in Cameroon in Africa.

**You now have one minute to study the question.**

**(m)** Bonjour, je m'appelle Jérôme et j'ai seize ans. Je suis élève au lycée franco-allemand dans le sud-ouest de l'Allemagne près de la frontière suisse. Notre prof de géographie a proposé à ma classe d'aider un enfant dans un pays pauvre. Nous avons contacté une organisation qui aide les enfants dans les pays en difficulté. Nous avons discuté pendant un mois et finalement nous avons choisi le Cameroun parce qu'on y parle français et nous pouvons ainsi écrire nos lettres en cours de français. Depuis juin dernier, nous correspondons avec un jeune camerounais, Harona, qui a 12 ans et qui habite un petit village où on parle français. Tous les mois, nous vendons des gâteaux à l'école pendant la récréation. Cet argent aide son village à acheter des vêtements et des médicaments. Nous voulons aussi offrir à Harona un appareil-photo avec lequel il pourra prendre des photos qu'il peut nous envoyer. Comme ça, nous pourrons mieux apprécier comment ils vivent dans son village. Nous espérons continuer cette amitié pendant longtemps.

*(2 minutes)*

**(t)** **Question number two.**

You then hear a programme about circuses in France.

**You now have one minute to study the question.**

**(m)** **or** **(f)** Le cirque est aujourd'hui moins populaire en France qu'il y a cinquante ans. Mais pendant l'été on voit toujours des affiches pour les cirques dans chaque ville, dans chaque petit village. C'est un monde magique, pour les enfants et leurs parents – un monde de musique, de lumières et de couleurs. Mais le cirque moderne a beaucoup changé. Par exemple, maintenant il y a beaucoup de cirques sans animaux sauvages. Dans le cirque moderne il y a beaucoup de disciplines telles que la danse. Mais tout a l'air d'être organisé comme l'était le cirque d'autrefois, surtout quand le cirque se déplace d'une ville à l'autre. Les gens du cirque se lèvent très tôt le matin, afin d'éviter les embouteillages et d'arriver à leur nouvel emplacement le plus rapidement possible. Une fois arrivés, ils prennent le déjeuner, et ils font une petite sieste avant le spectacle de l'après-midi à 14h 30. Quand celui-ci se termine, ils ont juste le temps de ranger leur matériel et de manger avant le spectacle du soir qui commence à 19h 30. Heureusement, il y a des villes où ils restent plusieurs jours. Ils en profitent pour faire les magasins ou se promener un peu en ville.

*(2 minutes)*

**(t)** **Question number three.**

You then hear an interview with 14-year old Laura who lives and works with her family in a circus.

**You now have one minute to study the question.**

**(f)** Salut! Je m'appelle Laura et j'ai 14 ans. J'habite dans une caravane avec mes parents et mon frère. Je suis contente car j'ai ma propre chambre où je peux jouer aux jeux vidéos. Mon père fait un spectacle avec des chevaux et ma mère est acrobate. Le matin avant d'aller à l'école, j'aide mon père à soigner les chevaux. Ils sont mignons – petits et blancs. J'ai aussi d'autres tâches. Par exemple je vends des glaces pendant l'entracte et je répare les costumes. Avant, je devais aller dans une nouvelle école à chaque fois que le cirque bougeait. J'avais des difficultés à m'adapter car les matières étaient souvent différentes et je n'avais pas toujours le temps de me faire des amis. Mais maintenant mon école est dans le cirque. Il y a un seul professeur qui voyage avec nous et les enfants de tous les âges sont ensemble dans la même classe. Et j'aime bien être avec les autres enfants du cirque. On est très proches car on vit et on travaille ensemble.

*(2 minutes)*

**(t)** **End of test.**

**Now look over your answers.**

*[END OF TRANSCRIPT]*

[BLANK PAGE]

FOR OFFICIAL USE

| | | | | | |
|---|---|---|---|---|---|

Mark

# X059/202

NATIONAL
QUALIFICATIONS
2011

TUESDAY, 17 MAY
10.30 AM – 11.00 AM
(APPROX)

FRENCH
INTERMEDIATE 2
Listening

---

**Fill in these boxes and read what is printed below.**

Full name of centre

Town

Forename(s)

Surname

Date of birth

| Day | Month | Year | Scottish candidate number | Number of seat |
|---|---|---|---|---|

When you are told to do so, open your paper.

You will hear three items in French. **Before you hear each item, you will have one minute to study the question.** You will hear each item three times, with an interval of one minute between playings, then you will have time to answer the questions about it before hearing the next item.

Write your answers, **in English**, in this book, in the appropriate spaces.

You may take notes as you are listening to the French, but only in this book.

You may **not** use a French dictionary.

You are not allowed to leave the examination room until the end of the test.

Before leaving the examination room you must give this book to the Invigilator. If you do not, you may lose all the marks for this paper.

DO NOT
WRITE IN
THIS
MARGIN

*Marks*

While in France, you are listening to the radio.

1.  You hear a talk by Jérôme, whose class has helped Harona, who lives in Cameroon in Africa.

    (*a*)  In which part of Germany does Jérôme live?  Mention any **one** thing.    1

    South - west of Germany

    (*b*)  Who suggested that his class should help someone in a poor country?    1

    His Geography teacher.

    (*c*)  Why did they choose to help someone in Cameroon?  Mention any **one** thing.    1

    Because its a french colony

    (*d*)  What age is Harona?    1

    17 years old

    (*e*)  How do the pupils raise money for their project?    1

    Recreation activities & Christmas

    (*f*)  What does the money buy?  Mention any **one** thing.    1

    (*g*)  Why do they want Harona to send them photos?    1

    To look at the life of the village

    *    *    *    *    *

Marks

2.    You then hear a programme about circuses in France.

   (a)    What makes the circus "a magical world"?  Mention any **two** things.     1

   _The music & the colours_

   (b)    In what ways has the modern circus changed?     2

   _The dancers are far more choreographed_

   (c)    Why do circus workers have to get up early when they move from town
          to town?  Mention any **one** thing.     1

   _to pick up the equipment_

   (d)    What do they do when they arrive in a new town?  Mention any **one**
          thing.     1

   _Have a short rest_

   (e)    What is the time of the evening performance?     1

   _19:30_

   (f)    What can they do if they stay in town for a few days?  Mention any **one**
          thing.     1

   _Go to the shops._

                  *     *     *     *     *

                        **[Turn over for Question 3 on *Page four***

*Marks*

3. You then hear an interview with 14-year old Laura who lives and works with her family in a circus.

   (*a*) Why does Laura like her bedroom? Mention any **one** thing.  1

   It's her own room

   (*b*) How does she help her father? 1

   She grows the horses

   (*c*) What other tasks does Laura do in the circus? Mention any **one** thing. 1

   Preparing the costumes

   (*d*) Why did Laura find it difficult always having to change schools? Mention **two** things. 2

   No time to make friends & different subjects

   (*e*) Her school is now in the circus. Why does she like this new arrangement? Mention any **one** thing. 1

\*    \*    \*    \*    \*

Total (20)

[END OF QUESTION PAPER]

# X059/204

| NATIONAL QUALIFICATIONS 2011 | TUESDAY, 17 MAY 11.20 AM – 12.00 NOON | FRENCH INTERMEDIATE 2 Writing |

20 marks are allocated to this paper.

You may use a French dictionary.

You are preparing an application for the job advertised below.

| | | |
|---|---|---|
| **Titre de Poste** | : | Vendeur/Vendeuse au rayon vêtements |
| **Profil** | : | Conseiller les clients, organiser les rayons |
| **Renseignements** | : | Pour plus de détails, contactez: |
| | | **M. Le Roux,**<br>Chef du rayon Prêt-à-porter<br>Carrefour<br>34000 Montpellier |

To help you to write your application, you have been given the following checklist of information to give about yourself and to ask about the job. Make sure you deal with **all** of these points:

- name, age, where you live
- leisure interests
- school/college career – subjects studied previously/being studied now
- reasons for application
- request for information about the job.

You could also include the following information:
- any previous links with France or a French-speaking country
- work experience, if any.

You have also been given a way to start and finish this formal type of letter:

**Formal opening to letter of application**

> Monsieur/Madame/Messieurs,
>
> Suite à votre annonce, je me permets de poser ma candidature pour le poste de . . .

**Formal finish to letter of application**

> En espérant que ma demande retiendra votre attention, je vous prie d'accepter, Monsieur/Madame/Messieurs, l'expression de mes sentiments distingués.

Use all of the above to help you write **in French** the letter which should be 120–150 words, excluding the formal phrases you have been given. You may use a French dictionary.

*[END OF QUESTION PAPER]*

**INTERMEDIATE 2 | ANSWER SECTION**

## FRENCH INTERMEDIATE 2
## READING
## 2007

**1.** (a) <u>Young students</u>/<u>young</u> people who are studying

(b) *Any two from:*
   - Speak <u>fluent</u> English/speak English <u>well</u> speak <u>good</u> English
   - (Be) (at least) 16 years old/(be) over 16/ minimum of 16
   - (Be) available (to work) in summer/free in the summer

(c) *Any one from:*
   - <u>Named</u> after a fish
   - (Is/has been) (totally) renovated/refurbished
   - (Has enough) places/space/room/seats for 10 (clients/customers)

(d) Vineyards/wine <u>and</u> climate/weather (*both elements are required*)

**2.** (a) • Cleaning <u>the cabin(s)</u>
   - Guided visits/guiding visitors/tour guide/tourist guide/visitor guide

(b) 30 hours or details (6 hours a day and 5 days a week (*Arithmetic will not be penalised if details are correct.*)

(c) <u>Walk</u> (<u>along</u>) <u>the canal</u>/<u>the river</u>/the length of the canal

(d) *Any one from:*
   - You will share a bedroom/cabin with <u>2(other)</u> <u>people</u>/ 2 others
   - Each cabin holds 3 people
   - There is a (small) kitchen (to prepare meals)

**3.** (a) *Any two from:*
   - <u>Build</u>/<u>pay</u> for stadiums/stadia
   - Build (new) roads
   - <u>Build</u> accommodation/lodgings/houses <u>for the athletes</u>

(b) (A lot of) traffic (problems)/(more) traffic/congestion

(c) *Any two from*
   - Encourages <u>young people</u>/<u>young ones</u>/ <u>youngsters</u>/<u>youth(s)</u> to <u>take up</u>/<u>practise</u>/ <u>participate</u> in <u>sport</u>
   - (Creates) (number of) (a lot of) jobs/ employment/employees
   - Reinforces/brings friendship <u>to each country that takes part</u>/participant <u>countries</u>

**4.** (a) *Any two from:*
   - <u>Online</u>/<u>Internet shopping</u>/buying online/groceries
   - <u>Communicate</u> with/<u>Speaking</u> to <u>friends on</u> (<u>your</u>) <u>computer</u>
   - Going abroad for <u>less than 5 euros</u>

(b) People who use their cars (in the centre of) <u>towns</u>/being able to drive in town

(c) *Any two from:*
   - They are crowded/overloaded/loaded/full/ cramped/lots of passengers
   - Dirty/filthy
   - (Often) late/delayed/it makes them late/they don't want to be late

(d) *Any one from:*
   - It (is a means of transport which) is clean/green

- (It allows you to do some) exercise

(e) Leave your car <u>in the car park</u>/<u>park</u> your car (around town) And then take the metro/subway/<u>underground</u> train/tube (*NB* park and ride = *1 point*)

(f) *Any one from:*
   - There is less noise
   - People <u>can walk safely</u>/it is less dangerous for <u>pedestrians</u>

(g) *Any one from:*
   - Breakdown(s)
   - <u>Medical</u> emergencies/urgencies/urgency

(h)

| Place | Reason |
|---|---|
| Restaurant | To describe what they are eating/what the food is like/to describe the food |
| Supermarket | To ask what to buy/what shopping they need |

(i) They <u>text</u>/<u>SMS</u>/<u>send texts</u>/<u>messages instead of</u> speaking/and don't speak <u>to him</u>

(j) *Any two from:*
   - (The ring tone/ringing) interrupt(s) the lesson/course/classes
   - The pupils lose their concentration/they break/affect/distract your concentration/stops the pupils concentrating
   - The pupils don't understand the lesson.

## FRENCH INTERMEDIATE 2 LISTENING 2007

1. (a) 5 km

   (b) *Any one from:*
   • She is lazy
   • They argue/fight (at lot/continually/often/all the time)/she is argumentative/we have disputes

   (c) (She is a) nurse

   (d) *Any one from:*
   • <u>Lays/prepares/sets</u> the table
   • <u>Makes/prepares/cooks</u> the <u>dinner/evening meal</u>/(high) tea/supper/Helps <u>by</u> preparing the dinner

   (e) She works as a waitress/server/waiter/<u>serves</u> in a restaurant

   (f) *Any two from:*
   • Puts it into (a) <u>bank</u> (account)/banks it
   • (Saves) for holidays/to go to Spain
   • (Buys) clothes
   • <u>Goes out with friends/nights out with friends</u>

   (g) *Any one from:*
   • It gives them experience <u>of work/work</u> experience
   • It makes them (very/more) independent/it means they have their own money to spend/they are independent

2. (a) (In the) <u>east</u> (of France)/(to the) east (of France)

   (b) In the morning the weather can be (**very**) **hot** at twelve/<u>very</u> warm but by 3 pm it can be **stormy/storms**/thunder <u>and</u> lightning (*both required*)

   (c) 2 <u>hours</u>

   (d) *Any two from:*
   • Medicine
   • Politics/Modern Studies
   • (Different/other/Modern/Foreign) languages

   (e) Ham <u>and</u> cheese/gammon <u>and</u> cheese (*both required*)

3. (a) Rodolphe taught pupils between the ages of **11** and **17** (*both required*)

   (b) *Any one from:*
   • <u>French</u> life/life in <u>France</u>/<u>French</u> culture/ <u>French</u> way of life/<u>French</u> lifestyles
   • <u>French</u> cinema/films

   (c) *Any one from:*
   • In a (youth) hostel
   • In a dorm/<u>room</u> with a (history) <u>teacher</u>

   (d) *Any one from:*
   • Castle<u>s</u>
   • Famous monument<u>s</u> ⎫ notion of
   • (Whisky) distillerie<u>s</u>/ ⎬ plural essential
   whisky factorie<u>s</u> ⎭

   (e) *Any one from:*
   • <u>Walked on the beach(es)</u> (*activity and place both required.*)
   • Trekked/walked/hiked in the <u>mountains/hills</u>/hill walking (*activity and place both required.*)
   • Took photos/pictures

   (f) (Too much) wind

## FRENCH INTERMEDIATE 2 WRITING 2007

**Task**
Letter of application for a job abroad, including information specified in a number of bullet points.

**Assessment Process**
1. The overall quality of the response will be assessed and allocated to a category/mark.
2. All 5 unavoidable bullet points should have been addressed. (There are 7 bullets, 2 of which include the words 'if any' and will not incur penalties if omitted.)
3. 2 marks will be deducted (ie single marks, not pegged ones) for each bullet not addressed, up to a maximum of 2 bullets. If 3 or more bullets have not been addressed, the mark will be 0.

(See pages 107–108 for descriptions of marking categories.)

**What if....?** *(instructions for markers)*

• *The candidate has failed to copy out the introductory section or has not adapted it to the correct gender?*
Pay minimal attention to this. However, it is an initial indication that the candidate probably will not attain the top mark.

• *Three bullet points fit into one category but two others are in the next, lower category?*
This is often an indication that you would award the higher category.
However, it may be wise to consider which bullet points are better. If the better sections include the first and second bullet points, which are more basic, you are less likely to be generous than if the final bullet points were of a better quality. You must look carefully at the quality of the candidate's work and then come to a decision. When in doubt give the candidate the benefit of the doubt.

• *The candidate very clearly is applying for an entirely different job to the one on the examination paper?*
The maximum award which can be given is 8/20, if the language is considered to be worth 12 or more.
If the language is assessed at 8, award the mark 4. Otherwise, award 0.

| Category/mark | Content | Accuracy | Language Resource – Variety, Range, Structures |
|---|---|---|---|
| *Very Good* 20 | • All five compulsory areas are covered fully, in a balanced way, including some complex sentences. <br> • Candidates cover the initial bullet points very correctly and competently but also provide detailed information in response to the later bullet points, which are specific to the job advert in question. <br> • A range of verbs/verb forms, tenses and constructions is used. <br> • Overall this comes over as a competent, well thought-out and serious application for a job. | • The candidate handles all aspects of grammar and spelling accurately, although the language may contain 1 or 2 minor errors. <br> • Where the candidate attempts to use language more appropriate to Higher, a slightly higher number of inaccuracies need not detract from the overall very good impression. | • The candidate is comfortable with the first person of the verb and generally uses a different verb or verb form in each sentence. <br> • Some modal verbs and infinitives may be used, especially at Bullet Point (BP) 5. <br> • There is good use of tenses, adjectives, adverbs and prepositional phrases and, where appropriate, word order. <br> • The candidate uses co-ordinating conjunctions and/or subordinate clauses, especially from BP 3. <br> • The language flows well. |
| *Good* 16 | • All five compulsory tasks are addressed, perhaps mainly using less complex sentences. <br> • The responses to bullet points 4 and 5 may be thin, although earlier points are dealt with in some detail. <br> • The candidate uses a reasonable range of verbs/verb forms. | • The candidate handles verbs accurately but simply. <br> • There are some errors in spelling, adjective endings and, where relevant, case endings. <br> • Use of accents is less secure. <br> • Where the candidate is attempting to use more complex vocabulary and structures, these may be less successful, although basic structures are used accurately. <br> • There may be one or two examples of inappropriately selected vocabulary, especially in the later bullet points. | • There may be repetition of verbs. <br> • Where relevant, word order is simple. <br> • There may be examples of listing, in particular at BP 3, without further amplification. <br> • There may be one or two examples of a co-ordinating conjunction, but most sentences are simple sentences. <br> • The candidate keeps to more basic vocabulary and structures in the final two bullet points and may only ask for one piece of information eg How much will I earn? |
| *Satisfactory* 12 | • The candidate uses mainly simple, basic sentences. <br> • The language is fairly repetitive and uses a limited range of verbs and fixed phrases, eg *I like*; *I go*; *I play*. <br> • Area 4 (reasons for application) may be covered in a rather vague manner. <br> • Area 5 (questions) may be addressed either with a general question or one single specific question, frequently about money or time off. | • The verbs are generally correct, but basic. <br> • There are quite a few errors in other parts of speech - gender of nouns, cases, singular/plural confusion. <br> • Prepositions may be missing eg I go the town. <br> • While the language may be reasonably accurate in the first three areas, in the remaining two control of the language structure may deteriorate significantly. <br> • Overall, there is more correct than incorrect. | • The candidate copes with the first and third person of a few verbs. <br> • A limited range of verbs are used on a number of occasions. <br> • Sentences are basic and mainly brief. <br> • There is minimal use of adjectives, probably mainly after 'is' eg Chemistry is interesting. <br> • The candidate has a weak knowledge of plurals. <br> • There may be several spelling errors eg reversal of vowel combinations. |

| Category and mark | Content | Accuracy | Language Resource – Variety, Range, Structures |
|---|---|---|---|
| *Unsatisfactory* 8 | • The content is basic. <br> • The language is repetitive, eg *I like, I go, I play* may feature several times within one area. <br> • As far as content is concerned, there may be little difference between Satisfactory and Unsatisfactory. <br> • While the language used to address BP 1 and 2 is reasonably accurate, serious errors appear during BP 3. | • Ability to form tenses is inconsistent. <br> • There are errors in many other parts of speech - gender of nouns, cases, singular/plural confusion. <br> • Several errors are serious, perhaps showing mother tongue interference. <br> • There may be one sentence which is not intelligible to a sympathetic native speaker. <br> • The final two areas may be very weak. <br> • Overall, there is more incorrect than correct. | • The candidate copes mainly only with the personal language required at BP 1 and 2. <br> • The verbs 'is' and 'study' may also be used correctly. <br> • Sentences are basic. <br> • An English word may appear in the writing. <br> • There may be an example of serious dictionary misuse. |
| *Poor* 4 | • The content and language are very basic. | • Many of the verbs are incorrect. <br> • There are many errors in other parts of speech - personal pronouns, gender of nouns, cases, singular/plural confusion. <br> • Prepositions are not used. <br> • The language is probably inaccurate throughout the writing. <br> • Three or four sentences may not be understood by a sympathetic native speaker. | • The candidate cannot cope with more than 1 or 2 basic verbs. <br> • The candidate displays almost no knowledge of the present tense of verbs. <br> • Verbs used more than once may be written differently on each occasion. <br> • Sentences are very short. <br> • The candidate has a very limited vocabulary. <br> • Several English words may appear in the writing. <br> • There are examples of serious dictionary misuse. |
| *Very Poor* 0 | • The content is very basic <br> **or** <br> • The candidate has not completed at least three of the core bullet points. | • (Virtually) nothing is correct. <br> • Most of the errors are serious. <br> • Very little is intelligible to a sympathetic native speaker. | • The candidate copes only with 'have' and 'am'. <br> • Very few words are correctly written in the foreign language. <br> • English words are used. <br> • There may be several examples of mother tongue interference. <br> • There may be several examples of serious dictionary misuse. |

# FRENCH INTERMEDIATE 2
# READING
# 2008

1. (a) *Any two from:*
   - Gardeners/gardening/working in gardens
   - Ice-cream sellers/vendors/selling ice-cream
   - Cooks/chefs/cooking jobs

(b

| 7 | Amusement/theme/fun parks in Europe |
|---|---|
| 4000 | Employees/workers/jobs |

)

   (c) All the activities/rides

2. (a) *Any one from:*
   - (when he was) 19
   - at Easter/during Easter Holidays

   (b) *Any one from:*
   - Distribute/give out sweets to children
   - Distribute/give out chocolate eggs/Easter eggs to children/eggs chocolate

   (c) *Any one from:*
   - (too) heavy
   - (he was) (always) thirsty/made him thirsty

   (d) *Any one from:*
   - Italian restaurant open from/at/after/for midday/noon
   - Park closing in 15 minutes

   (e) Good relationships/connection with colleagues/got on well/had a good rapport with colleagues/fellow workers/good relation(s) with colleagues

3. (a) •  Healthier/more healthy menu/meals/ lunches/diet/eating/food
   - They have a healthy menu now
   - Can use IT/computing room(s) on Sundays

   (b) *Any one from:*
   - Learn to live together/to get on well together/with others/to live well together
   - To discourage violence/to decrease violence/to stop violence

   (c) *Any two from:*
   - Give seat to older person/offer their place to old(er) person/the elderly
   - Say hello/greet the driver/say good morning/hi to the driver
   - Don't throw ticket on the ground/floor/don't litter with ticket

4. (a) *Any two from:*
   - Training/coaching (a) football (team)/football trainer/taking (a) football (team)
   - Working with sick animals
   - Visiting disabled/handicapped people/ person/the handicapped

   (b) First experience of the working (world)/first experience of work/world of work *(NB first experience of a job is needed)*

   (c) *Any one from:*
   - Who will walk the dog when it rains/ is raining/in the rain?
   - Where will we/you leave the dog when we go on holiday?

   (d) *Any one from:*
   - (Its) accommodation/housing/lodging/ home/kennel
   - (Its) food/nourishment

   (e) *Any one from:*
   - Birthday card(s)
   - Sticker(s)

   (f) (For) 10 years

   (g) *Any two from:*
   - Feed them/give them something to eat
   - Clean their cage
   - Play with them

   (h) *Any two from:*
   - No running water
   - (Children were in) classes of 50 (pupils)/(students)
   - (A lot of) people were ill because there were not a lot/enough doctors/hardly any doctors

   (i) *Any one from:*
   - Sell (UNICEF) products in French cities/towns
   - Organise/host/set up shows/sporting events

   (j) *Any two from:*
   - Build hospitals
   - Feed the children
   - Create/produce/build schools in the villages

   (k) *Any one from:*
   - Send/give/donate/clothes/books/ games/toys/send their clothes

## FRENCH INTERMEDIATE 2 LISTENING 2008

1. (a) Michelle Durand    ✓

   (b) If you have questions/she/he can answer your questions/problems if you have a question/to ask questions/queries

   (c) 35

   (d) 8 euros/€8/about £7

   (e) Any one from:
   - 3 bedrooms
   - small kitchen
   - you can prepare/make breakfast

   (f) Near/close to/next to the (park) exit/just before you leave the park

   (g) Any two from:
   - Red cap/hat (with name of park)/Cap/hat with name of park
   - Yellow tee-shirt
   - Black trousers
   - Cap/hat, tee-shirt and trousers
   - Red, yellow and black

2. (a) 15 (different) nationalities

   (b) Any two from:
   - (Always) arrive on time/be punctual/do not be late
   - no (drinking) alcohol
   - no smoking

   (c) Any one from:
   - Explore the park
   - Visit/go to/swim in the swimming pool/go swimming

   (d) Any one from:
   - Go to night club/disco/clubbing
   - Go shopping/visit shops/there are shops

   (e) Every half hour/30 minutes/2 every hour (until 1 o'clock in the morning)

3. (a) Maths

   (b) Any one from:
   - Going/touring round world
   - To improve/perfect/correct his English
   - To work on a farm

   (c) Any one from:
   - Strange/funny/weird/bizarre/unusual/unique animals/wildlife/the animals were different
   - Smiling people

   (d) Any one from:
   - Insects in bathrooms
   - Snakes/serpents under the bed

   (e) Any one from:
   - Mountainous/mountains
   - Island
   - Eat more fruit and vegetables (than Belgians)

   (f) Any one from:
   - Take advantage of the good weather
   - Sunbathe/get a tan
   - Visit historic sites/places/parts/areas

## FRENCH INTERMEDIATE 2 WRITING 2008

**Task**

Letter of application for a job abroad, including information specified in a number of bullet points.

**Assessment Process**

1. With reference to *Content*, *Accuracy* and *Language Resource*, the overall quality of the response will be assessed and allocated to a pegged mark.

2. All 5 unavoidable bullet points should have been addressed. (There are 7 bullets, 2 of which include the words 'if any' and will not incur penalties if omitted.)

3. 2 marks (ie single marks, not pegged ones) will be deducted for each bullet not addressed, up to a maximum of 2 bullets. If 3 or more bullets have not been addressed, the mark must be 0.
   (See answers to 2007 Writing paper on pages 106–108 for descriptions of marking categories and responses to 'What if..?' questions.)

## FRENCH INTERMEDIATE 2
## READING
## 2009

1. (a) The Eurostras organisation is looking for students aged between **14** and **20.**

   (b) *Any one from:*
   - March/Next March/from March
   **OR**
   - Next year/this coming year

   (c) In a youth hostel/in youth hostels

   (d) • Make/design/draw a (small) poster/a notice
   - Explain why <u>your school</u> should/deserves to/must participate/take part/should be chosen

2. (a) *Any one from:*
   - Introduce/present <u>themselves</u> in <u>French</u>
   **OR**
   - Meet/talk with the other participants/meet the others/contestants

   (b) *Any two from:*
   - Food
   - Flag**s**
   - Post card**s**

   (c) (i) It is <u>made of</u>/constructed <u>from</u> glass
   (ii) Talk about/discuss/debate <u>European</u>/<u>EU</u> politics/policy

   (d) (The one) able to/can collaborate/work <u>best</u> <u>in a team/best</u> <u>teamwork</u>/whose <u>team</u> worked <u>the best</u>/the best working team

3. (a) • <u>Walked</u> in/around <u>the roads/streets/walked</u> <u>around town</u>
   - Bought souvenirs/present**s**/gift**s** for his family

   (b) *Any one from:*
   - They/the groups had/there was a party/celebration/they celebrated
   **OR**
   - They sang songs in <u>every/all/different/each/their own language</u>

   (c) He had to say goodbye to/he was leaving/parting from/losing his <u>new friends</u>/the friends he had made

   (d) Created/made/built a garden <u>in their school</u>

4. (a) *Any two from:*
   - What am I going to do/will I do <u>after</u> <u>school</u>?/when I leave school?
   - Where am I going to/will I live/stay?
   - Am I going to/will I find a job?

   (b) *Any two from:*
   - He has his <u>own</u> room
   - His room is on the ground/bottom floor
   - His room is well equipped/equipt/has everything you need

   (c) *Any one from:*
   - He had to share them/it (with the other students)
   **OR**
   - He had to wait a long time (to get washed)/students took a long time (to shower)

   (d) (i) She washed (his) clothes/did (his) laundry/washing/linen

   (ii) Cooked/made (him) <u>good</u>/nice meal**s**/food

(e) *Any one from:*
   - He made (some) friends/he got friends
   **OR**
   - Went out more/started to go out (with friends)

(f) (i) He gives/does/teaches/runs/takes <u>Spanish</u> lessons/courses/classes

   (ii) *Any two from:*
   - The rent/to pay for his flat
   - The bill**s**/invoice**s**
   - Leisure/free-time/spare-time (activities)/hobbies

(g) *Any one from:*
   - You learn how to manage/organise/look after (your) money
   - You have <u>more</u> freedom/liberty/independence

(h) *Any one from:*
   - He would(n't) eat <u>correctly/properly/well/the correct/</u> <u>right</u> food
   - He would get lost <u>in a</u> (big) <u>city/town</u>

(i) *Any one from:*
   - He calls/phones her/she hears from him <u>once a week/every week</u>
   - He gives her news/he tells her the news/she gets all the news <u>once a week/every week</u>

(j) It is (very) important <u>to like/to love</u> the place/area you are going to live (for a few years)/to make sure you like it first

# FRENCH INTERMEDIATE 2
# LISTENING
# 2009

1. (a) *Any one from:*
   - (In the centre of) Geneva (any recognisable spelling)
   **OR**
   - Switzerland

   (b) • It is (a bit) difficult
   - The <u>teacher</u> is (very) boring/the teachers are boring/the teacher doesn't make it interesting

   *Any two from:*

   (c) • (It) helps her to relax/it is relaxing/calming/lets out her stress
   - (It) helps her lose/get away from/<u>forget</u>/<u>not to think about</u> her problems
   - she can draw/design <u>for</u> the/does artwork/painting <u>for</u> the school magazine

   (d) *Any one from:*
   - Family <u>problem(s)</u>/problem(s) at home/family issues
   **OR**
   - <u>How to get</u> better/good grades/marks (in school)

   (e) • <u>Impoverished</u>/<u>poor</u> children('s charity/association) children in poverty/children from a <u>poor</u> background

2. (a) Two weeks/15/14 days/a fortnight

   (b) (i) <u>Her friend</u> had forgotten/didn't bring his/her/their passport/couldn't find her/his passport

   (ii) (Because of the) fog/mist

   (c) *Any one from:*
   - It was dirty/not clean/had not been cleaned
   **OR**
   - It had no fridge

   (d) *Any one from:*
   - (Went) swimming/swam <u>in the pool</u>/went in the pool
   - Played cards <u>on the terrace/patio</u>

   (e) *Any two from:*
   - <u>She</u> fell off (the bike)
   - She <u>broke</u> her leg/fractured <u>her</u> <u>leg</u>
   - She had to go to/went/ended up <u>in hospital</u>/they took her <u>to hospital</u>

3. (a) 3 <u>am</u>/3 <u>in the morning/at night</u>

   (b) *Any two from:*
   - Clothe<u>s</u>/cloths/clothing
   **OR**
   - Computer<u>s</u>
   **OR**
   - Alcohol/booze/drink

   (c) • They were wearing jeans, a black **jumper(s)/pullover(s)/sweater/jersey** and **white** trainers.

   (d) *Any one from:*
   - In a <u>green</u> lorry/van/truck
   **OR**
   - (Through/out/by the) (underground) car park/parking lot/the car park exit
   **OR**
   - (Through/out/by the) basement

   (e) • 03-88-20-**54-16**.

# FRENCH INTERMEDIATE 2
# WRITING
# 2009

**Task**

Letter of application for a job abroad, including information specified in a number of bullet points.

**Assessment Process**

1. With reference to *Content, Accuracy* and *Language Resource*, the overall quality of the response will be assessed and allocated to a pegged mark.

2. All 5 unavoidable bullet points should have been addressed. (There are 7 bullets, 2 of which include the words 'if any' and will not incur penalties if omitted.)

3. 2 marks (ie single marks, not pegged ones) will be deducted for each bullet not addressed, up to a maximum of 2 bullets. If 3 or more bullets have not been addressed, the mark must be 0.

(See answers to 2007 Writing paper on pages 106–108 for descriptions of marking categories and responses to 'What if..?' questions.)

## FRENCH INTERMEDIATE 2 READING 2010

1. (a) • Twins
   • 12 years old

   (b) *Any one from:*
   • Leaving for/Going to <u>US(A)</u>, <u>America next year</u>
   **or**
   • To speak/talk (English) <u>with the children</u>/help <u>the children with English</u>

   (c)

   | | |
   |---|---|
   | Your bedroom must be kept clean | |
   | You will have the main bedroom | |
   | Your bedroom is next to the children's | ✓ |
   | You will have to share the bathroom | ✓ |

2. (a) • Every day <u>except</u> Wednesday and Sunday/not on Wednesday and Sunday

   (b) • Help with homework
   • Look after/occupy/be in charge of/entertain them/ keep them busy <u>when/if the parents go out/we go out</u>

   (c) *Any one from:*
   • Ironing
   • <u>Help</u> to prepare/make (the) meal<u>s</u>/food/cooking

   (d) *Any one from:*
   • French <u>lesson(s)/course(s)/class(es)</u>
   • <u>Look around/walk in</u> the <u>neighbouring/nearby</u> areas/districts/<u>neighbourhood</u>/quarter

3. (a) • The language/French <u>is spoken</u> (everywhere)/ The main language is French/The majority speak French
   • <u>Historic</u> buildings/<u>dating from that time</u>

   (b) *Any one from:*
   • Sun(ny)(practically) <u>all year/always/all the time/ every year</u>
   • Warm welcome (from the people)/friendly people/population/welcoming

   (c) *Any two from:*
   • Beautiful coast(line)/the coast is/the coasts are beautiful
   • <u>Traditional fishing</u> villages
   • Busy/<u>Lively</u> town<u>s</u>/cities

4. (a) *Any one from:*
   • To <u>forget</u> work/studies/school
   • To get away/escape from everyday/daily life/get a break from their normal life

   (b) *Any one from:*
   • Split up with <u>boy</u>friend
   • Was ill (for a few months)

   (c) • Spain for a week (**need both parts**)

   (d) *Any two from:*
   • Relax/rest/unwind
   • Read
   • Get a tan/sunbathe

   (e) *Any two from:*
   • <u>Too many</u> people/tourists/<u>too</u> busy
   • No <u>room</u>/place for her towel/nowhere <u>to</u> put her towel/nowhere to sit
   • Got (painful) sunburn/sunstroke/heat stroke/too much sun

   (f) *Any two from:*
   • Food was bad/not good/not nice
   • <u>Couldn't sleep</u> because of <u>noise</u> (from nightclubs)/ <u>noise kept her awake</u>/because of the nightclub
   • Mosquito(es) <u>biting/stinging</u> her

   (g) *Any one from:*
   • (Afraid) to leave the house <u>empty/no-one</u> to look after the house
   • No one to <u>water</u> the garden/flowers

   (h) (Read about it) in a <u>magazine/an article</u>

   (i) *Any three from:*
   • They have all the comfort(s) of a home/house/all mod cons
   • Away from/far from tourists/there are no tourists (nearby)
   • Find out about/get to know/become acquainted with/meet other families (living in the neighbourhood/nearby)/get to meet another family
   • Children never get bored

   (j) (Only) have to <u>pay/buy</u> the plane/flight ticket/ agency fees

## FRENCH INTERMEDIATE 2 LISTENING 2010

1. (a) • 16

   (b) • Same age/both 16
      • Things/Lots in common/Same interests/like(d) the same things/stuff/hobbies/(both) like(d) fashion/(both) fashionable

   (c) • (Her) family <u>and</u> (her) town/city/where she lives

   (d) *Any one from:*
      • Teachers are **more/very** understanding (in Great Britain)/Teachers are **less** understanding **in France**
         **or**
      • They/The pupils have **less** homework (in Great Britain)/Pupils have **more** homework **in France**

   (e) • Played cards/a card game
         **or**
      • Talked about difference between <u>the</u> (two) countries/ France and England/France and (Great) Britain

   (f) • Study (foreign) language<u>s</u>

2. (a) *Any one from:*
      • (Too) young/not old enough/young girl
         **or**
      • (Too) dangerous/not safe (on her own)/she could get hurt

   (b) *Any one from:*
      • She keep in touch/contact/phone/speak (to them) <u>every day/always/all the time</u>
         **or**
      • <u>Help</u> (her aunt) with the housework/chores

   (c) *Any one from:*
      (i) • She had to be in by 21:00/9 (p.m./in the evening/at night)/Was not allowed out after 9
            **or**
         • Couldn't/wasn't allowed to invite friend(s) to the house/have friend(s) round/over/stay over

      (ii) • She <u>found/leased/ rented/got/moved into/decided to stay in</u> a flat/apartment/ house/home <u>with (her new)</u> (boy) <u>friend(s)</u>

   (d) *Any one from:*
      • Sold ice creams/ice cream seller/vendor/server
         **or**
      • Works at/a job <u>at/on</u> the beach/seaside

   (e) *Any one from:*
      • <u>First</u> experience/time <u>without</u> (her) <u>parents</u>
         **or**
      • Experience of <u>life/real world/travelling without</u> (her) <u>parents</u>
         **or**
      • (Got more/Gained/grew in) (self-)confidence

3. (a) • A year ago/last year

   (b) • He worked in a <u>nursery (school)/preschool</u>/day care/<u>Kindergarten/crèche</u>
      • with children between **3** and **6** years old

   (c) *Any one from:*
      • Games/play/sport(s)/play time
         **or**
      • Songs/singing/singalong

   (d) • They were poor/didn't have a lot of/had little money/poor living conditions/can cope without money/didn't have a lot
      • They were (always) smiling/happy/cheerful/ positive/live happily/have a good spirit

   (e) • You get to know/learn about/are more aware of a country/the inhabitants
         **or**
      • About a country/how others live/what the people are like/about the inhabitants/lifestyles/what it is like to live there

## FRENCH INTERMEDIATE 2
## WRITING
## 2010

**Task**

Letter of application for a job abroad, including information specified in a number of bullet points.

**Assessment Process**

1. With reference to *Content, Accuracy* and *Language Resource*, the overall quality of the response will be assessed and allocated to a pegged mark.

2. All 5 unavoidable bullet points should have been addressed. (There are 7 bullets, 2 of which include the words 'if any' and will not incur penalties if omitted.)

3. 2 marks (ie single marks, not pegged ones) will be deducted for each bullet not addressed, up to a maximum of 2 bullets. If 3 or more bullets have not been addressed, the mark must be 0.

(See answers to 2007 Writing paper on pages 106–108 for descriptions of marking categories and responses to 'What if..?' questions.)

## FRENCH INTERMEDIATE 2
## READING
## 2011

1. (a) • 12 years ago

   (b) *Any one from:*
   • Pedestrian precinct/zone/area/pedestrianised zone/street
   • <u>Two minutes</u> (on foot) from/to the town hall/ mayor's office/town house

   (c) *Any two from:*
   • Well equipped/good equipment/well fitted
   • Air-conditioned/conditioning
   • <u>In</u> a historic building

   (d) *Any one from:*
   • Host families/family/with a family
   • (Youth) hostel(s)

2. (a) • Lessons take place all year except <u>bank/public holidays</u>

   (b) *Any two from:*
   • Listening
   • Reading
   • Writing

   (c) *Any two from:*
   • <u>Call/phone</u> (SNCF/train) station about (train) times/timetables/schedules/information
   • <u>Get/Buy</u> (fresh) <u>produce/products/food at the market</u>
   • Make/take an <u>appointment</u> at the doctor's/arrange to meet the doctor/try to get the doctor

3. (a) *Any one from:*
   • (Take time) to relax/unwind/rest
   • Go out with/(Take time) to see friend**s**/spend time with friend**s**

   (b) • (They have) been ill/unwell/sick <u>during the year</u>
   • They <u>have been</u> unwell

   (c) • Cut/mow/do grass/lawn(s) (for neighbour)
   • Walk dog(s) <u>for neighbours</u>

   (d) *Any one from:*
   • (Buy) (a new) computer(s)
   • (Pay for) a holiday(s) <u>abroad/foreign</u> holiday(s)

4. (a) *Any one from:*
   • Spend day/time at lake(side)/loch
   • Throw bread to/at/for the ducks/feed the ducks

   (b) • No school on Wednesday/the next day

   (c) (i) • Made <u>sand</u> castle(s)
       (ii) • Read him/**her**/tell him/**her** a story

   (d) (i) *Any two from:*
       • (Doesn't like) the way/how she dresses/clothes/fashion
       • (Doesn't like) the jewellery (she wears)
       • Thinks she's <u>too young</u> to wear make-up
       (ii) • As if she were still 8 years old

   (e) • They become closer (again)/she will still be close to them/get along <u>better</u>

   (f) • Cleaning/Chores/Housework/housekeeping **and** the garden

   (g) (i) • Teaches/shows him how to use a computer/helps him with the computer/internet
       (ii) • His <u>shopping online/on the Internet</u>
       • Skype/Speak/communicate <u>with his nephew in USA/America</u>

(*h*) *Any two from:*
- (At the table) he had to sit up straight/upright/properly/sit right (on his chair)
- Never/don't interrupt/disrupt conversation(s)
- Not allowed to/never dared to speak about his tastes in music

(*i*) *Any one from:*
- (Loves) speaking about the things that interest them/their interests
- (Loves to) advise them/give advice when they have problems/helps with their problems/talks about their problems

# FRENCH INTERMEDIATE 2 LISTENING 2011

1. (*a*) *Any one from:*
   - South west
   - <u>Near/at/on</u> Swiss border/Switzerland

   (*b*) • <u>Geography</u> teacher

   (*c*) *Any one from:*
   - They speak French (there)/They speak the same language/It's a French country
   - Can write letters <u>in French</u> (class)/can write <u>in French</u>

   (*d*) • 12

   (*e*) • Sell/bake cakes (during interval)/home-baking/bake sale/gateaux

   (*f*) *Any one from:*
   - Clothes/Cloths
   - Medicine(s)/medication/medical care/medical help
   - Camera (for Harona)

   (*g*) • They can appreciate (better) how they live (in his/her village)/see what life is like in the village/see what the village is like/see what situation Harona is in/learn about village life

2. (*a*) *Any two from:*
   - Music/musical
   - Light/lighting
   - Colour(s)/colourful

   (*b*) • (Many without/have) no/fewer (wild) animals (now)/there used to be animals
   - (Includes other acts/disciplines such as) dance/dancing

   (*c*) *Any one from:*
   - (to) avoid traffic (jams)/there is a lot of traffic/the roads get busy
   - (to) get/arrive there as quickly/early as possible/so they are there quicker/so they can get quickly to another town/promptly

   (*d*) *Any one from:*
   - Have lunch/dinner/something to eat/food/a meal
   - (Have a) rest/siesta/nap/sleep

   (*e*) • 19.30/7.30(pm)/half 7

   (*f*) *Any one from:*
   - Shop(ping)/go to the shops/buy things from the shop
   - Walk/around (the town)/sightsee (around the town)/walk into town

3. (*a*) *Any one from:*
   - Her <u>own</u> room
   - She can play video <u>games</u>/her (games) console/ PS2/3/her room/it has video games

   (*b*) • (with/looks after/cares for/grooms/cleans/brushes/feeds/prepares) horse<u>s</u>/gets horse<u>s</u> ready (for performances)

   (*c*) *Any one from:*
   - Sells ice cream (during interval)
   - <u>Repairs/fixes/sorts</u> costumes

   (*d*) • Subjects/classes/lessons/work/courses (were often) <u>different/new</u>/difficult to <u>adapt to subjects</u>
   - (No time) to make friends/doesn't make a lot of friends/couldn't make friends/had to make (new) friends

(*e*) *Any one from:*
- Only one teacher/teacher travels with them/has the same teacher/she's always in the same class
- The children/they are all together in one class/she likes being with the other children/she can be with the other children/children of all ages in her class/there are other circus kids in school
- They <u>live</u> and <u>work</u> together

# FRENCH INTERMEDIATE 2 WRITING 2011

**Task:**

Letter of application for a job abroad, including information specified in a number of bullet points.

**Assessment Process:**

1. With reference to *Content, Accuracy and Language Resource*, assess the overall quality of the response and allocate it to a pegged mark.

2. Check that all 5 unavoidable bullet points have been addressed. (There are 7 bullets, 2 of which include the words "if any" and will not incur penalties if omitted.)

3. Deduct 2 marks (ie single marks, not pegged ones) for each bullet not addressed, up to a maximum of 2 bullets. If 3 or more bullets have not been addressed, the mark must be 0.

(See answers to 2007 Writing paper on pages 106–108 for descriptions of marking categories and responses to 'What if..?' questions.)

Hey! I've done it

© 2011 SQA/Bright Red Publishing Ltd, All Rights Reserved
Published by Bright Red Publishing Ltd, 6 Stafford Street, Edinburgh, EH3 7AU
Tel: 0131 220 5804, Fax: 0131 220 6710, enquiries: sales@brightredpublishing.co.uk,
www.brightredpublishing.co.uk

Official SQA answers to 978-1-84948-198-4
2007-2011